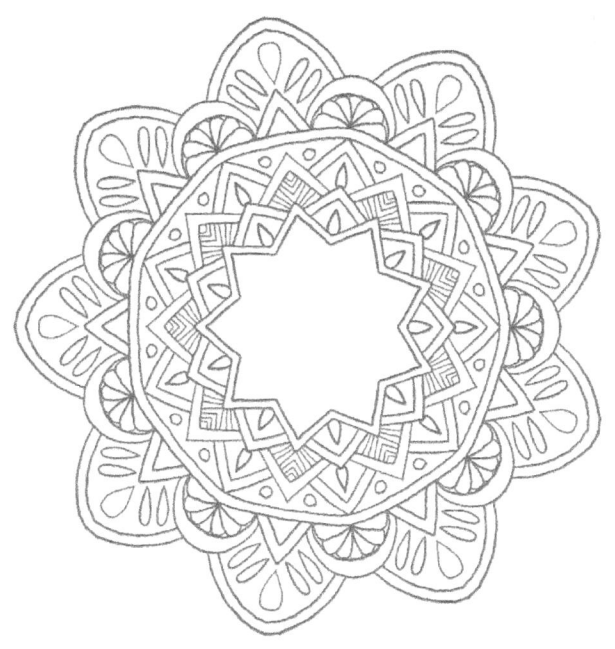

THIS BOOK BELONGS TO

_____

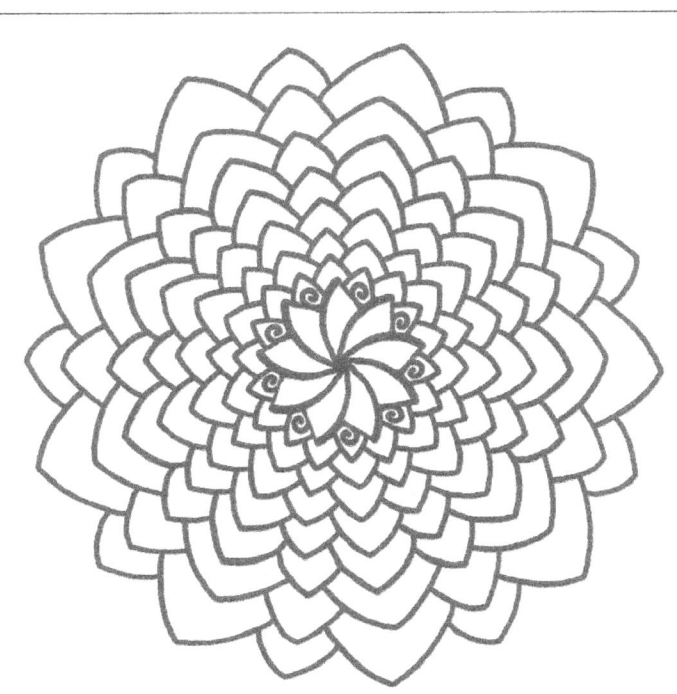

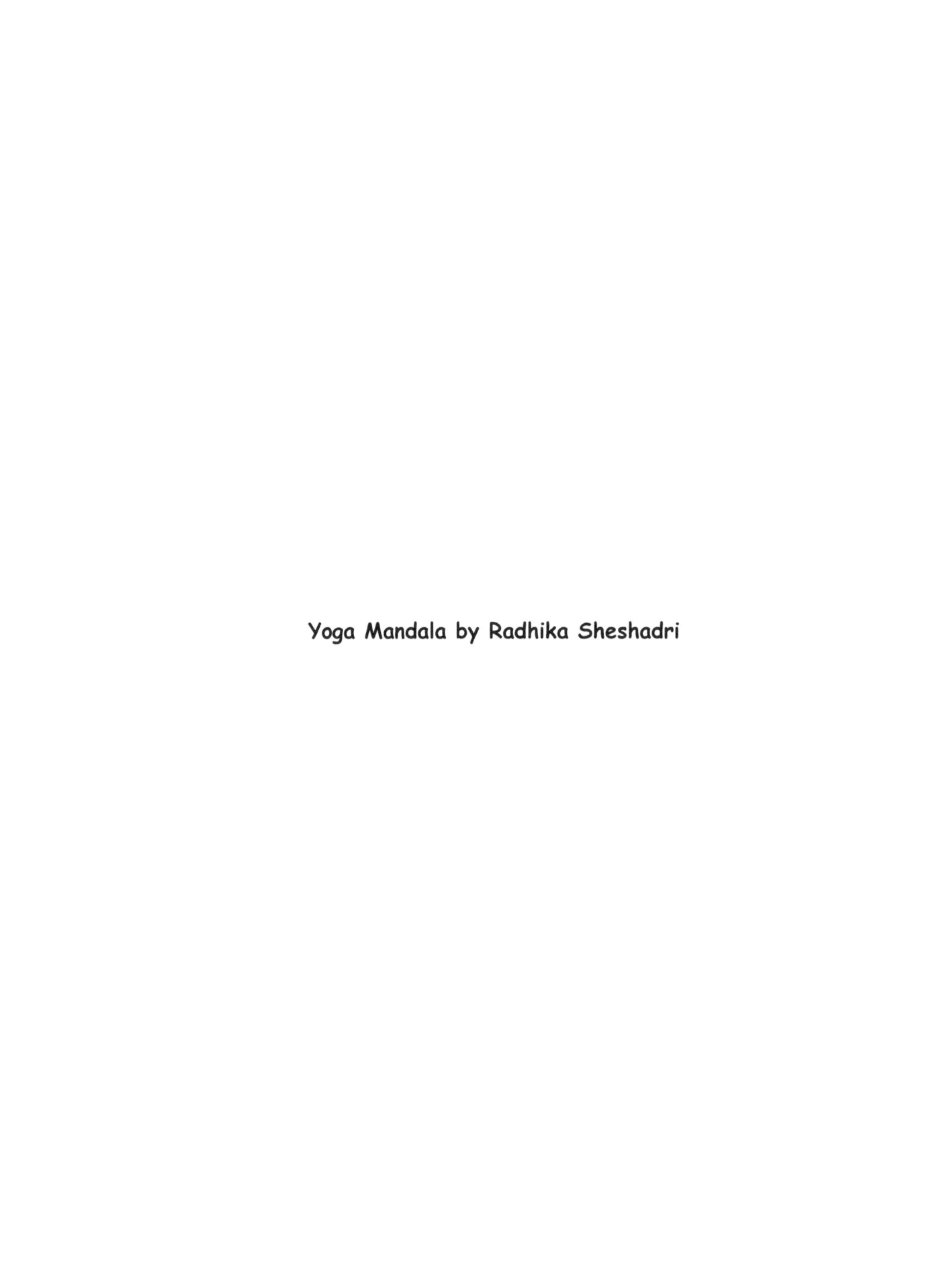

Yoga Mandala by Radhika Sheshadri

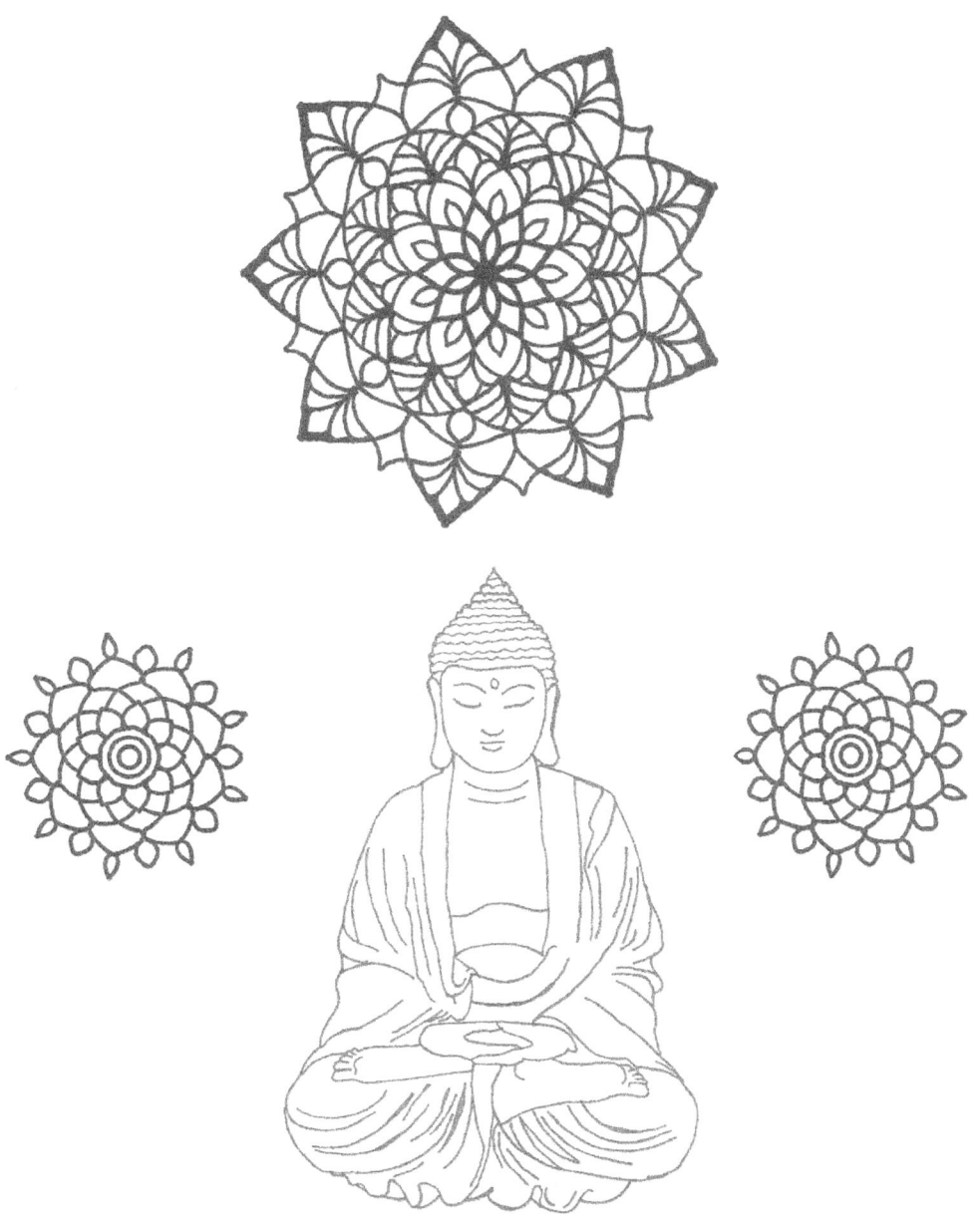

Radiate boundless love towards the
entire world. ~The Buddha

Yoga Mandala by Radhika Sheshadri

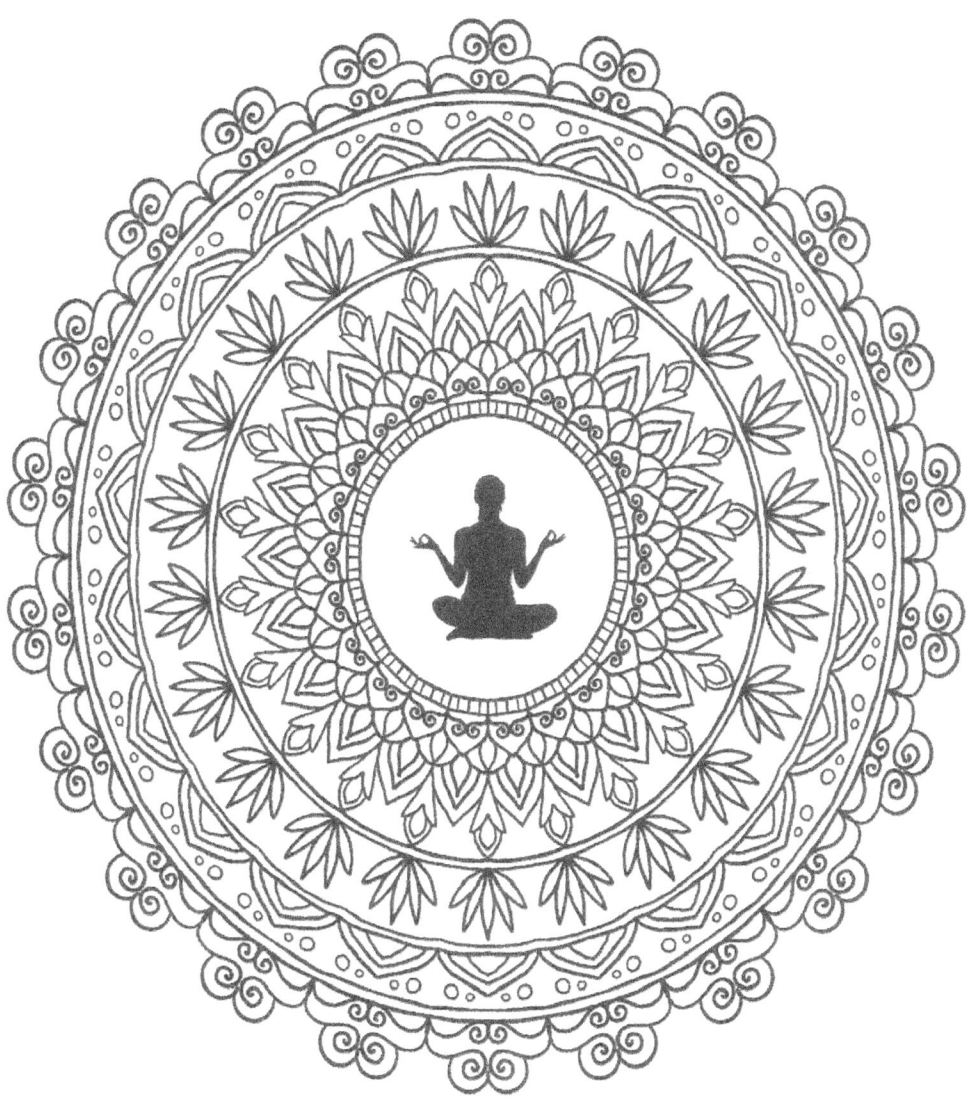

Peace comes from within. Do not
seek it without.~ The Buddha

Yoga Mandala by Radhika Sheshadri

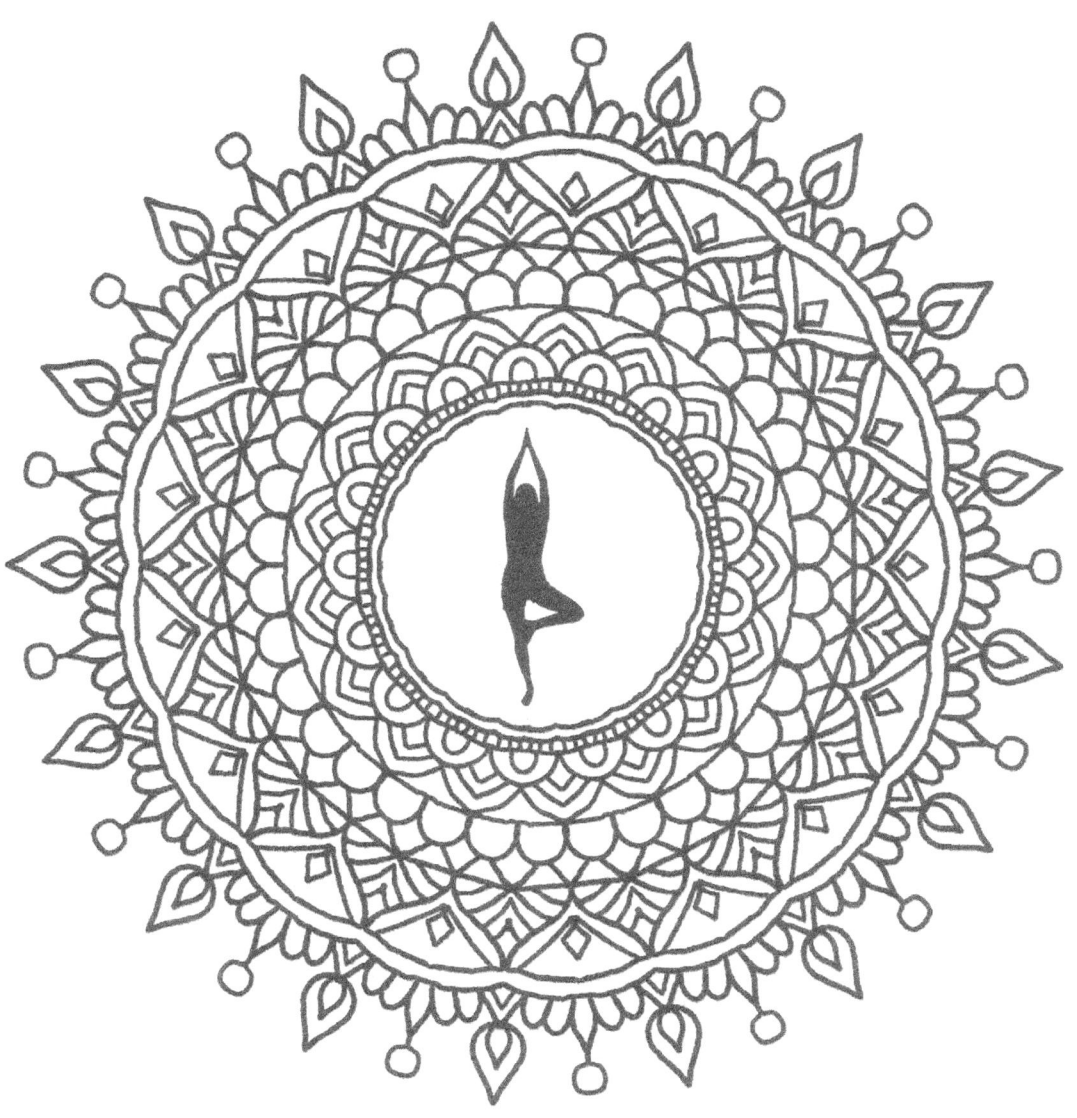

You, yourself, as much as anybody in the entire universe, deserve your love and affection.~ The Buddha

Yoga Mandala by Radhika Sheshadri

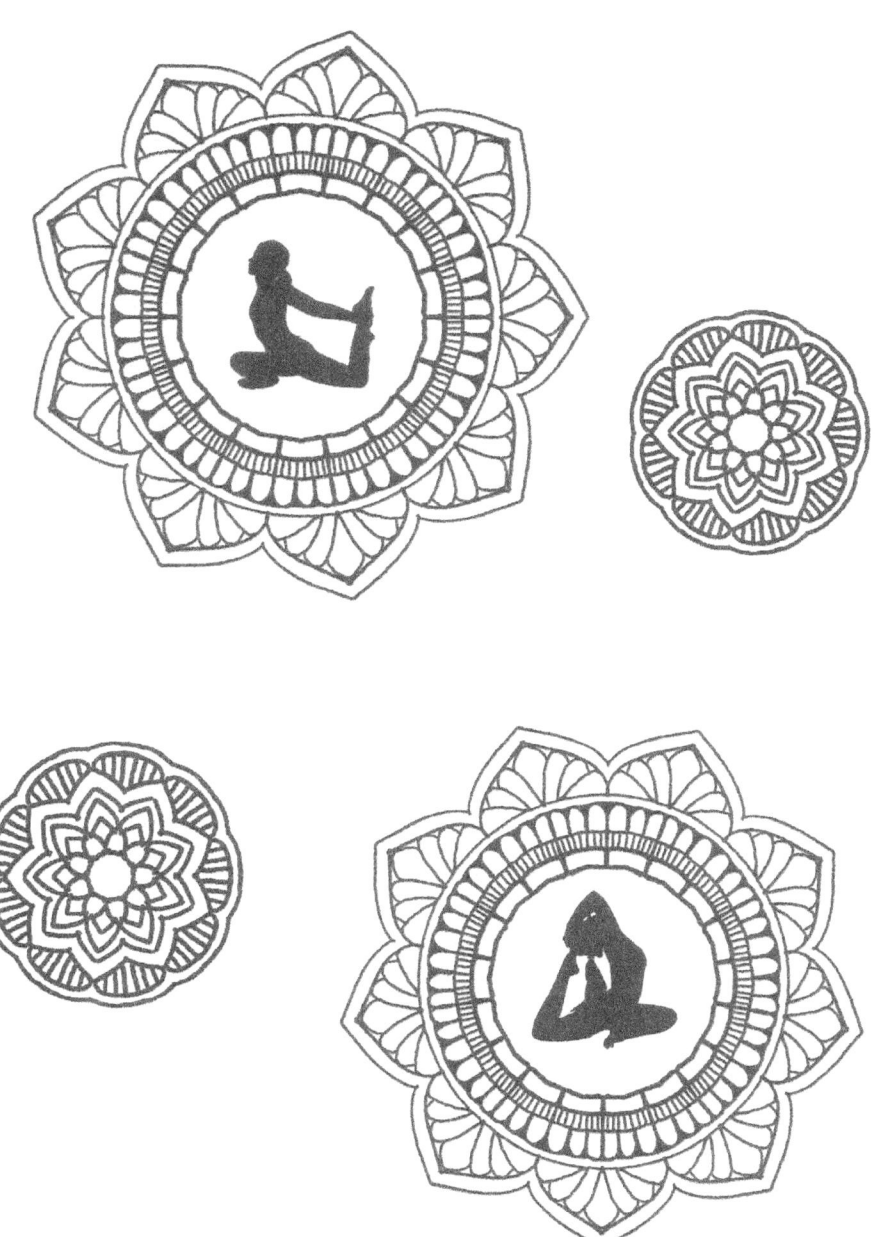

It is better to travel well than to
arrive. ~The Buddha

Yoga Mandala by Radhika Sheshadri

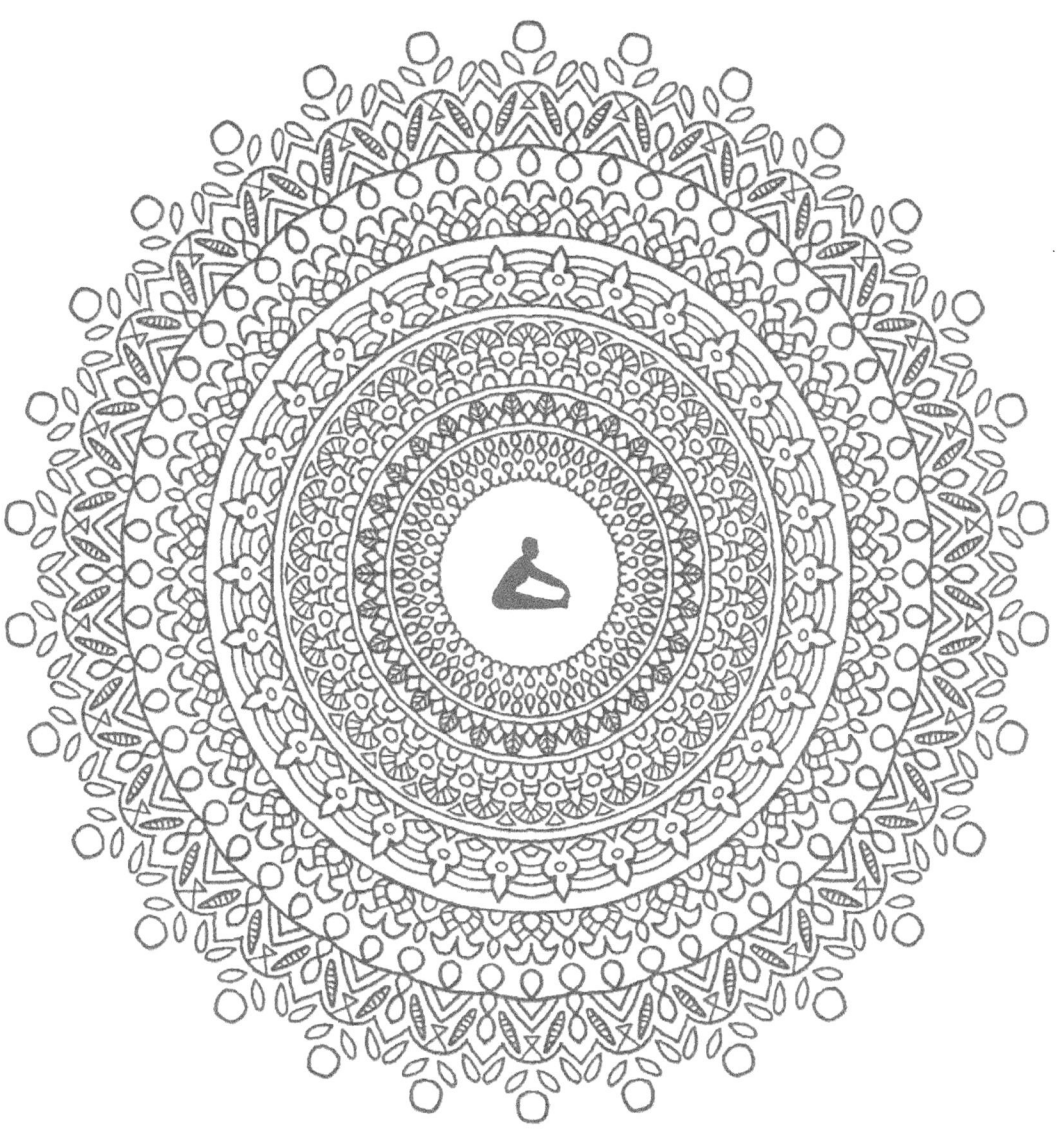

I do not dispute with the world; rather it is the world that disputes with me.~The Buddha

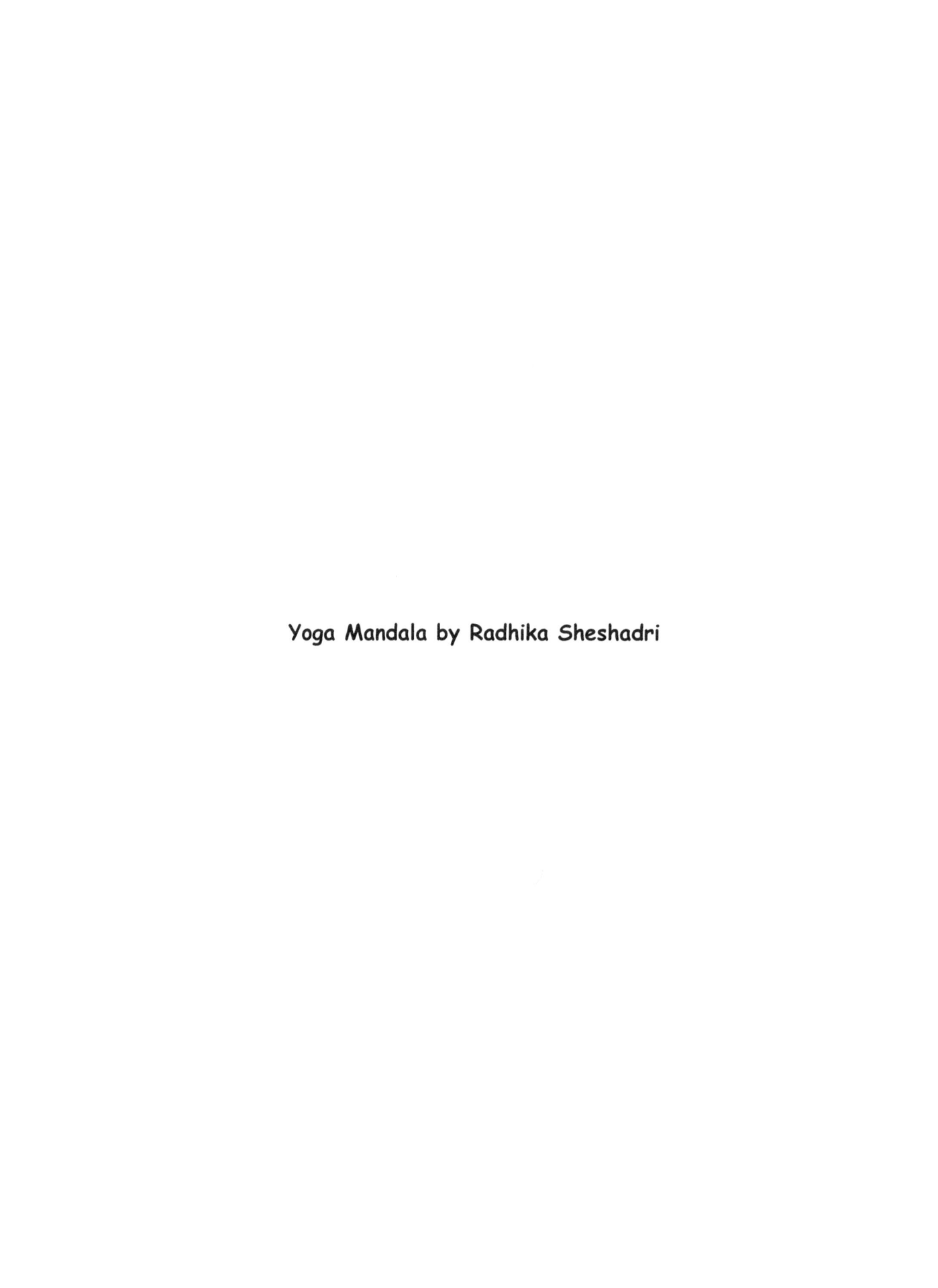

Yoga Mandala by Radhika Sheshadri

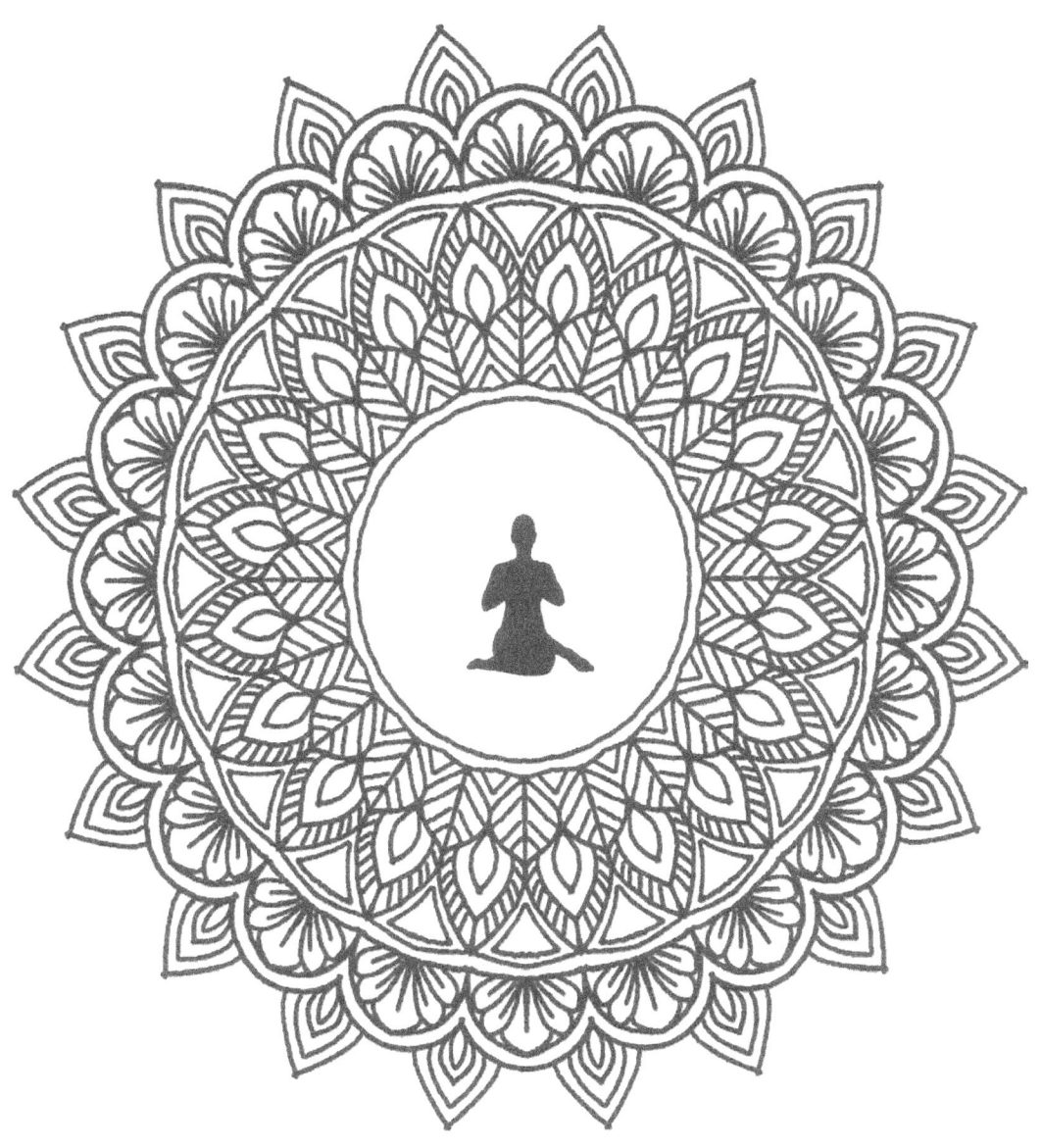

Do not overrate what you have received, nor envy others. He who envies others does not obtain peace of mind. ~ The Buddha

Yoga Mandala by Radhika Sheshadri

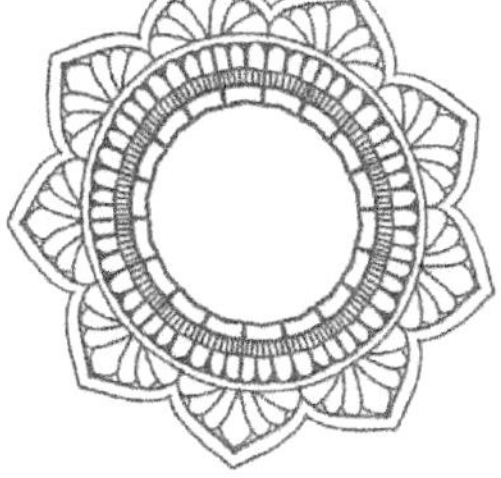

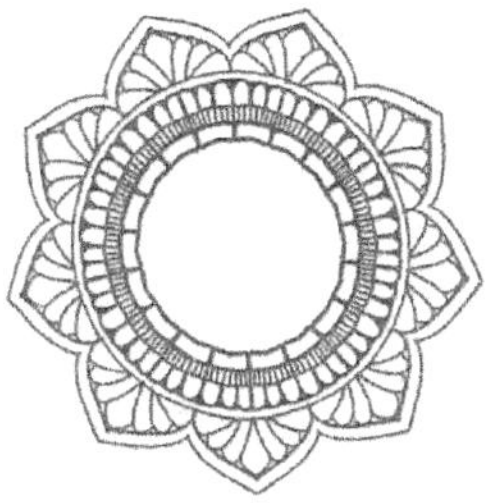

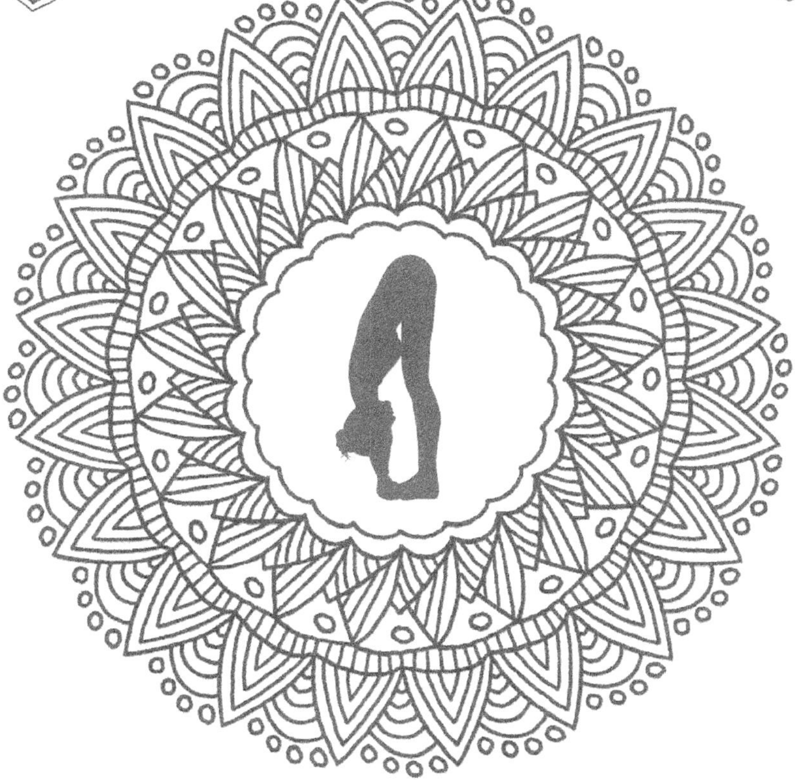

It is a man's own mind, not his enemy or foe,
that lures him to evil ways. ~The Buddha

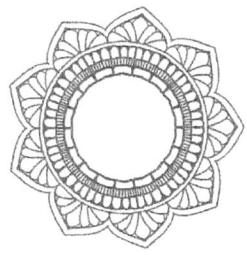

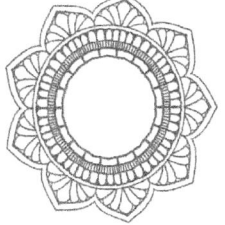

Yoga Mandala by Radhika Sheshadri

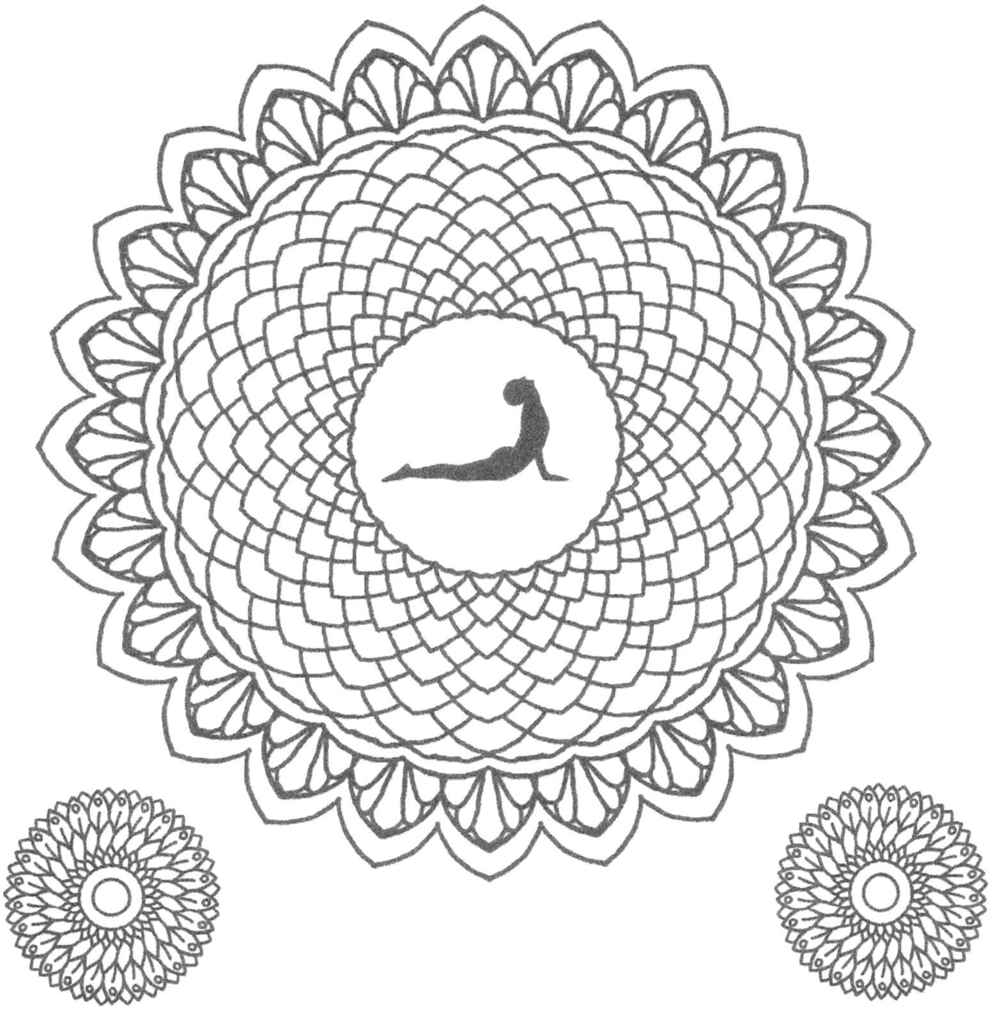

Just as a candle cannot burn without fire, men cannot live without a spiritual life. ~The Buddha

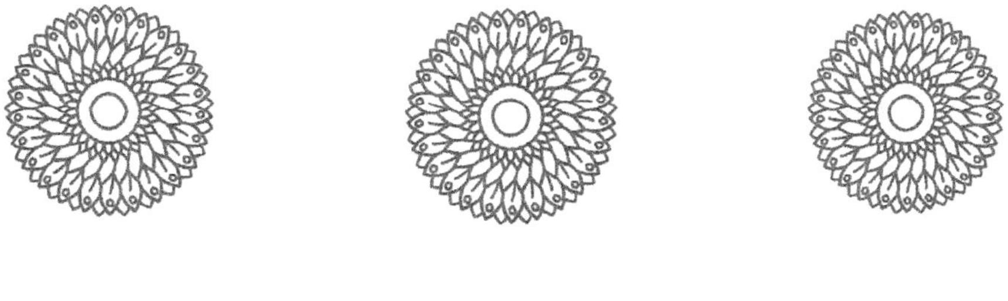

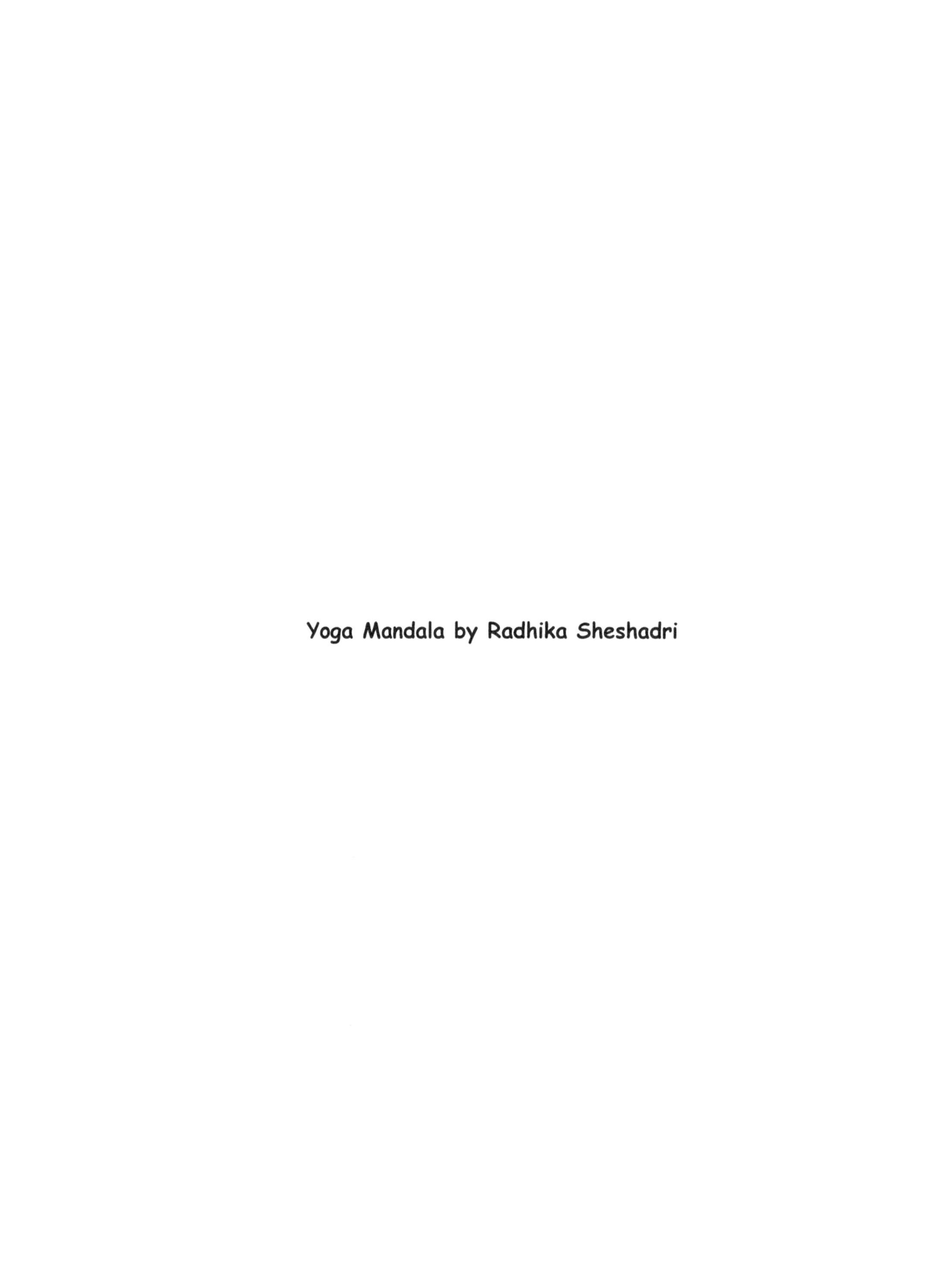

Yoga Mandala by Radhika Sheshadri

Work out your own salvation. Do not depend on others. ~The Buddha

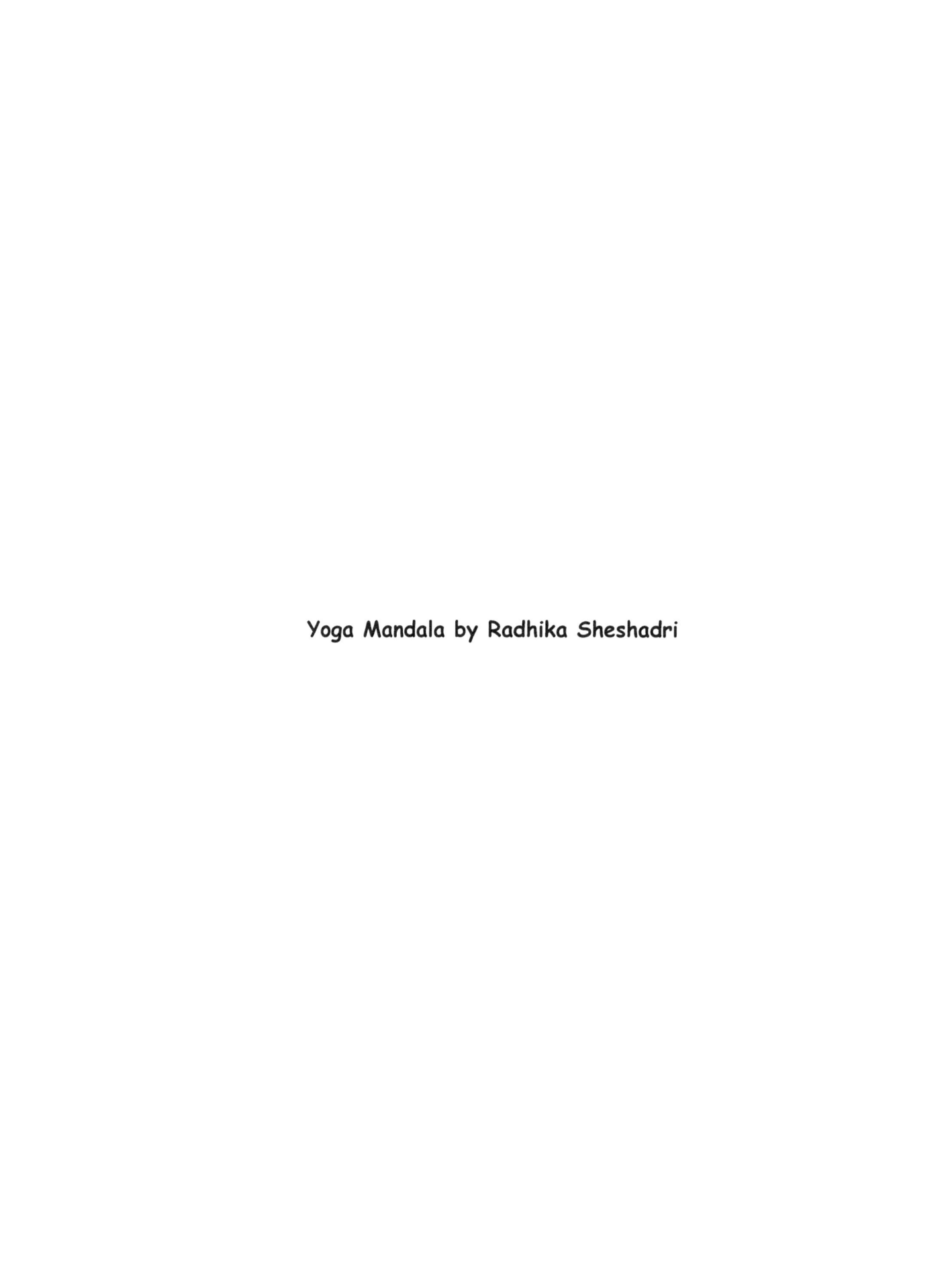

Yoga Mandala by Radhika Sheshadri

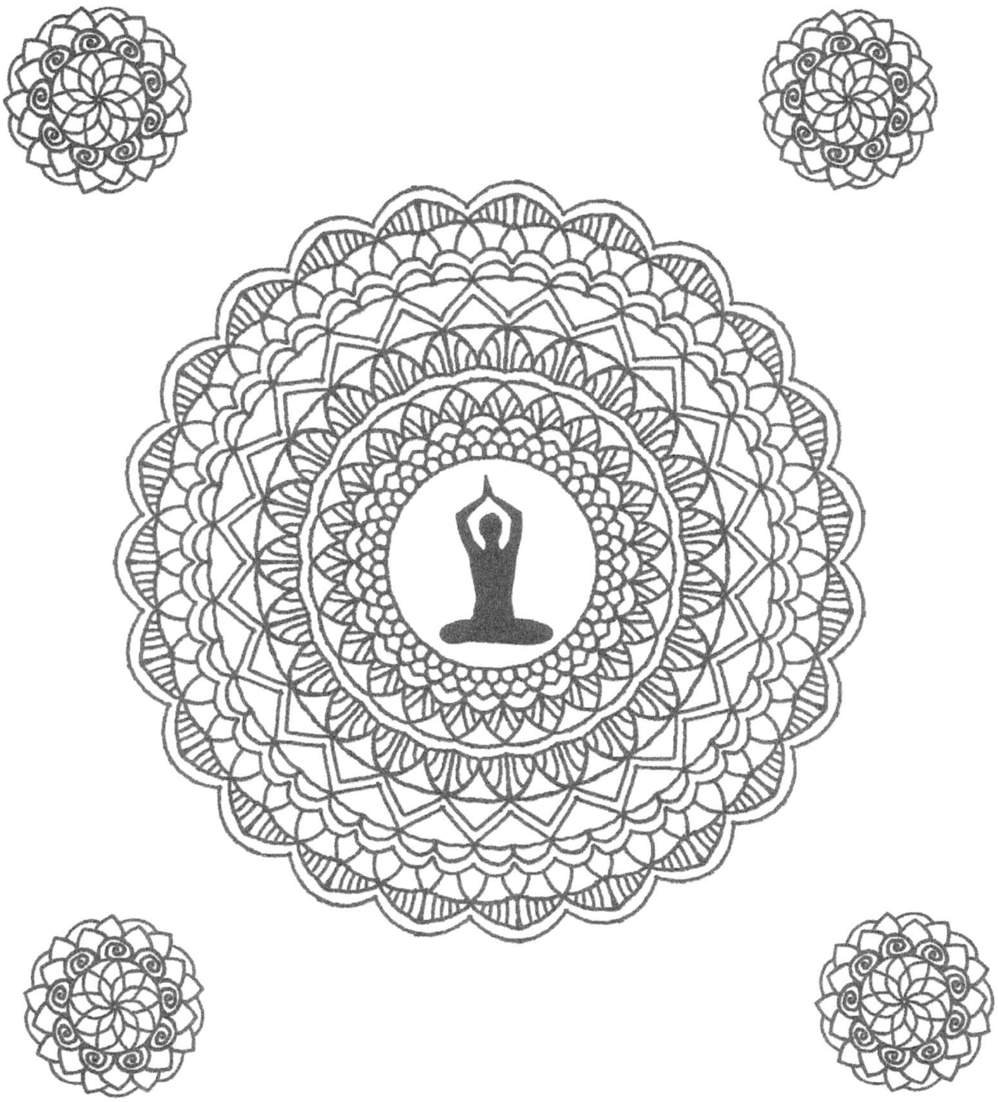

Health is the greatest gift, contentment the greatest wealth, faithfulness the best relationship. ~The Buddha

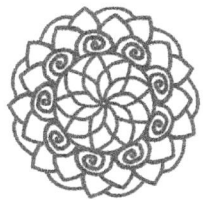

Yoga Mandala by Radhika Sheshadri

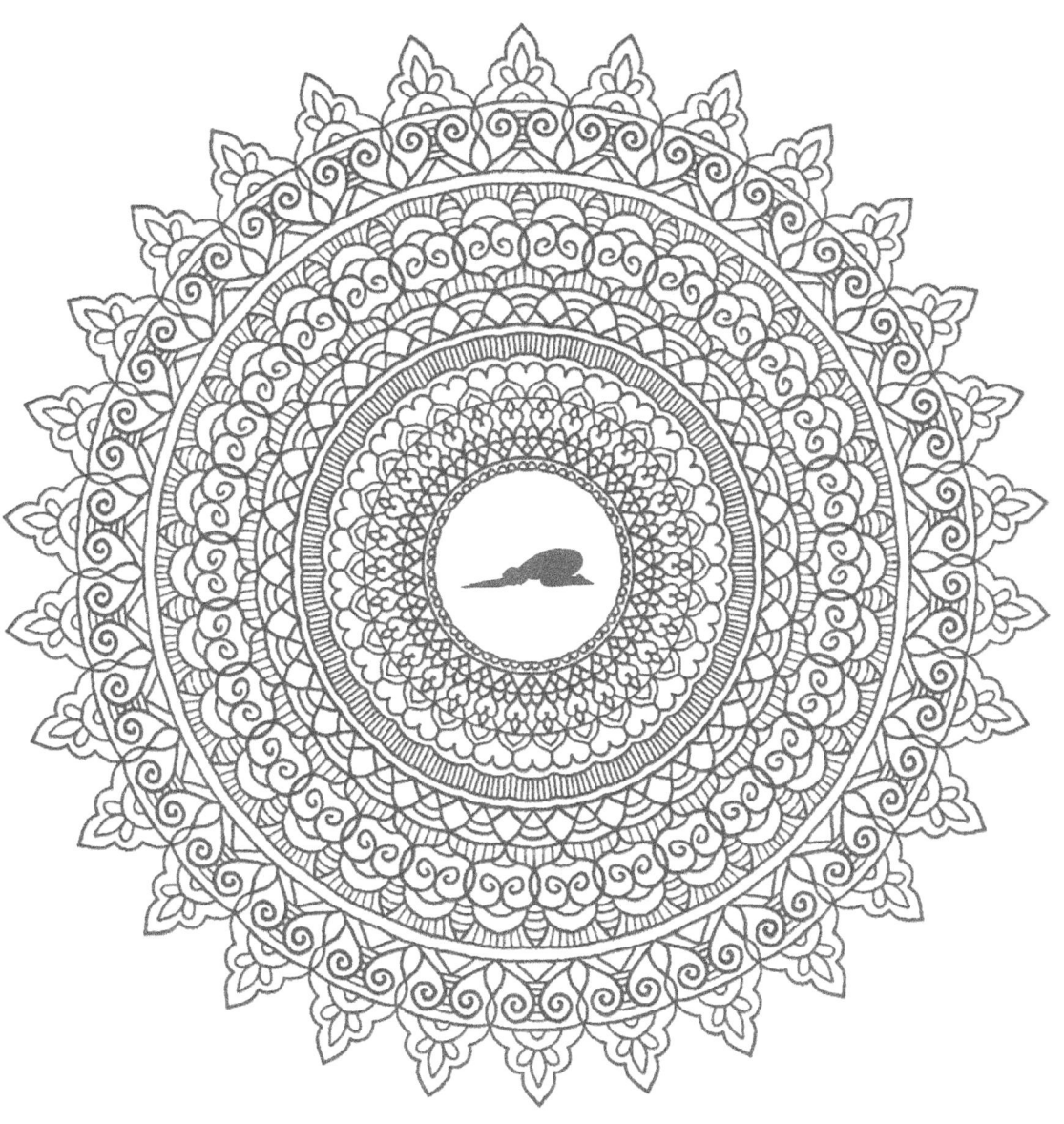

The Way is not in the sky; the Way
is in the heart. ~ The Buddha

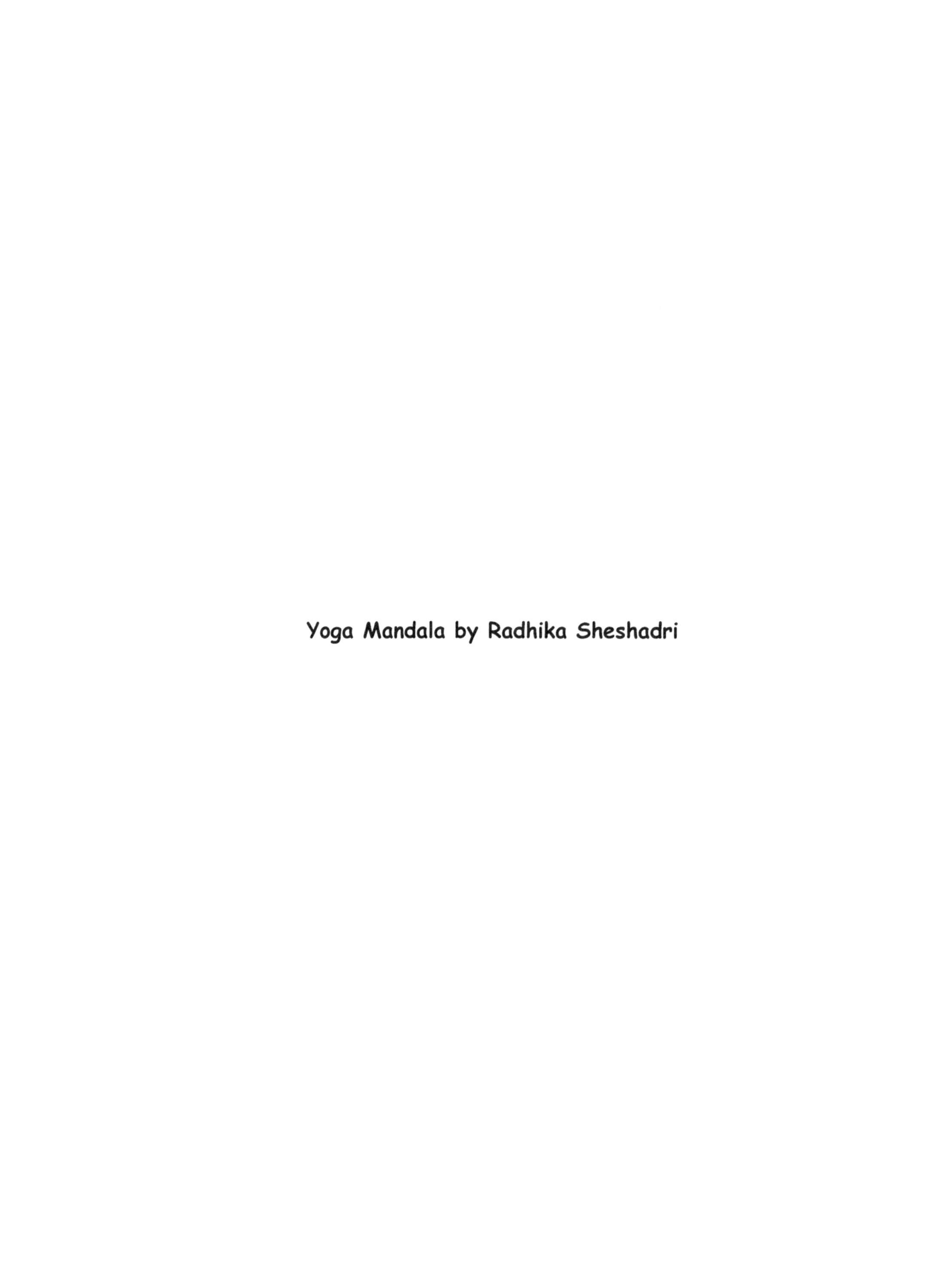

Yoga Mandala by Radhika Sheshadri

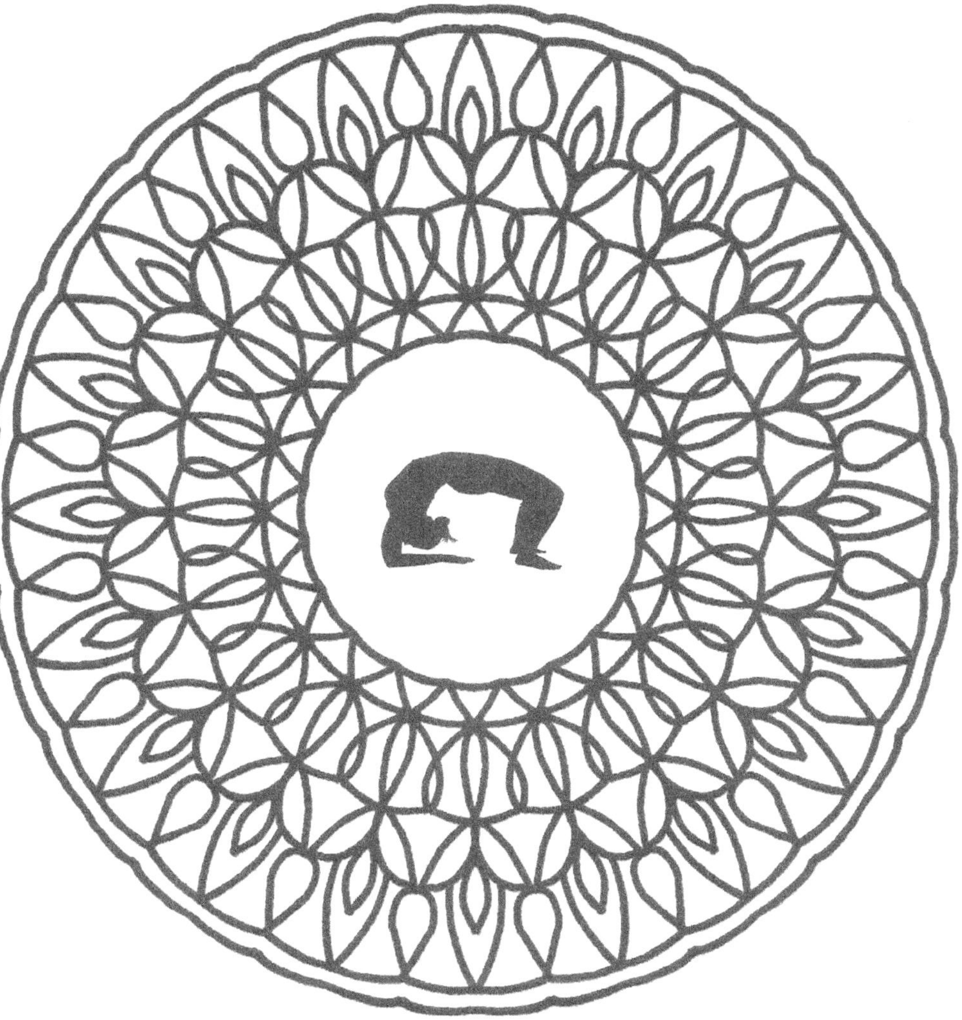

Even death is not to be feared by one
who has lived wisely. ~The Buddha

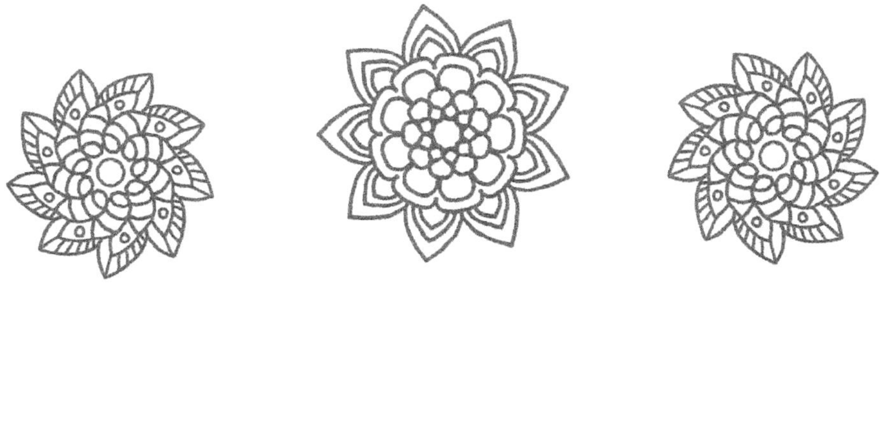

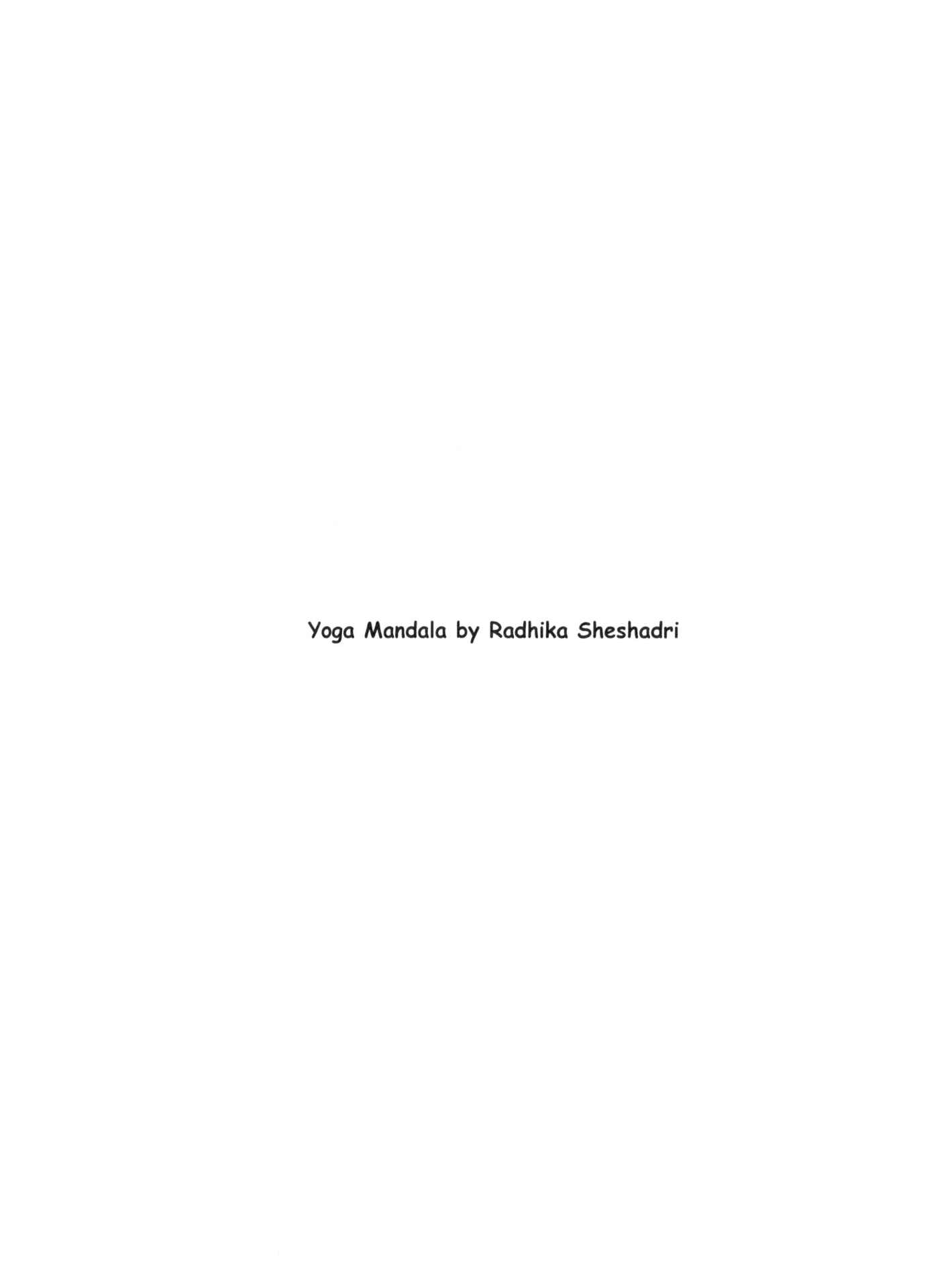

Yoga Mandala by Radhika Sheshadri

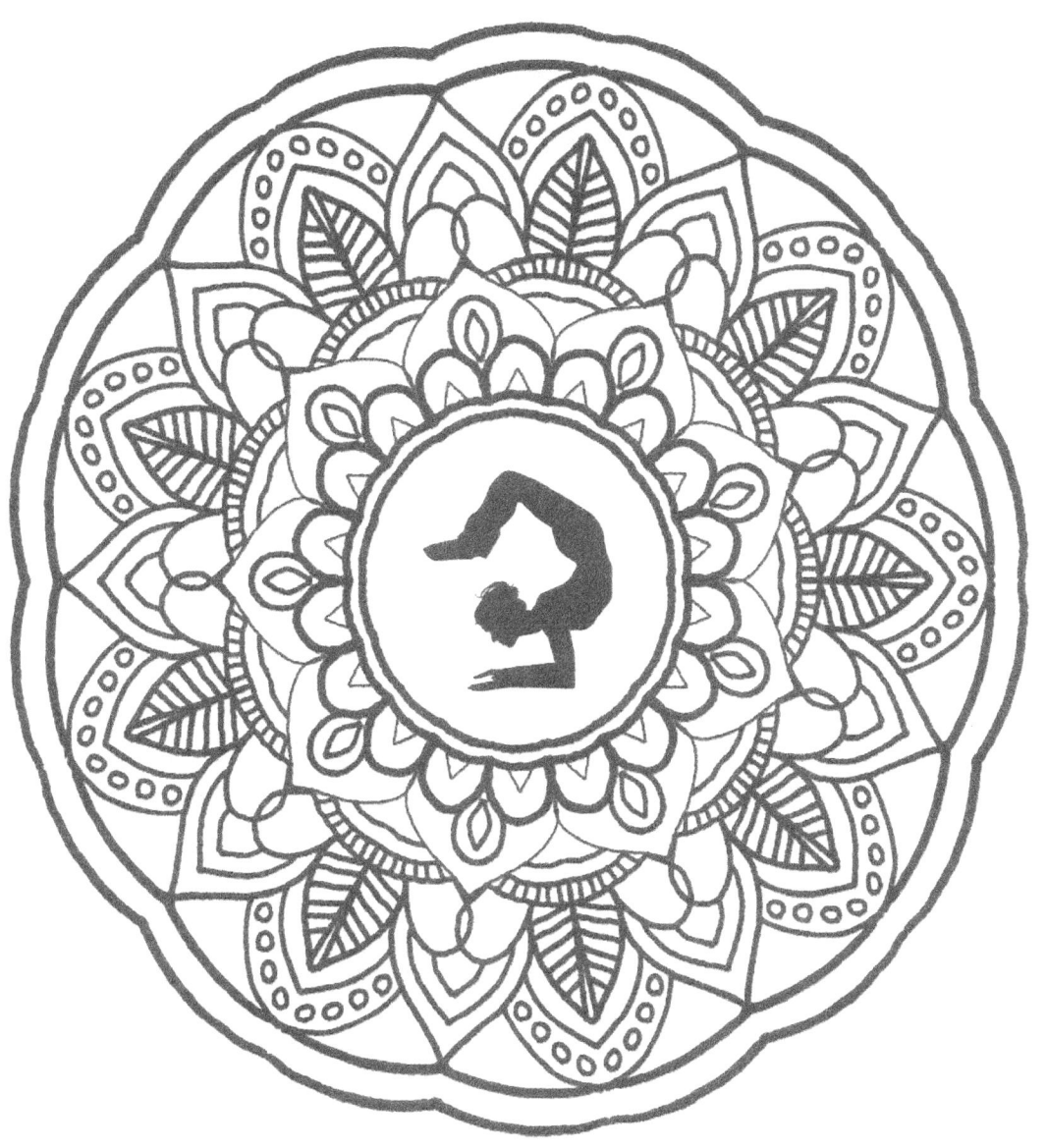

Three things cannot be long hidden: the sun,
the moon, and the truth. ~The Buddha

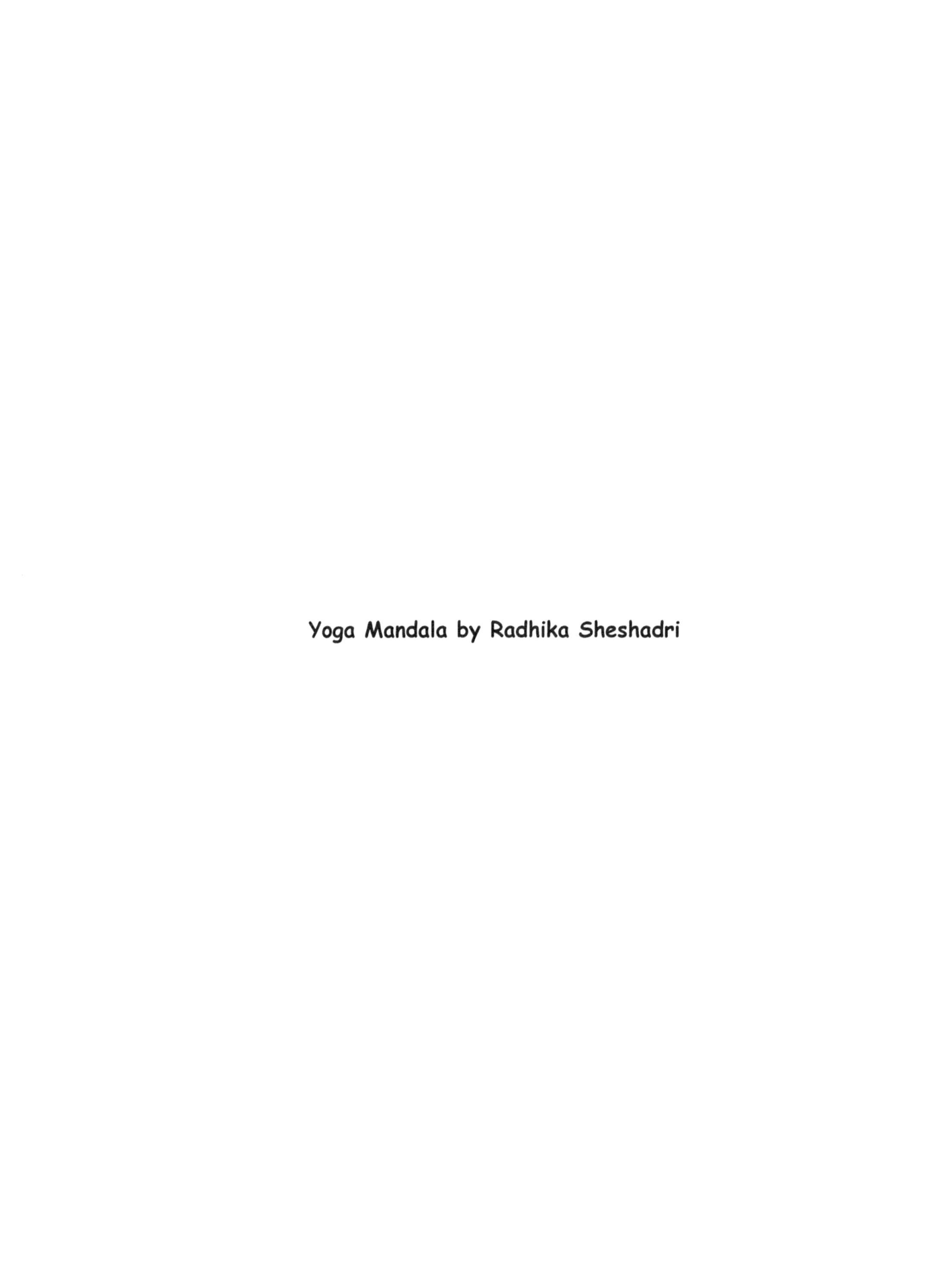

Yoga Mandala by Radhika Sheshadri

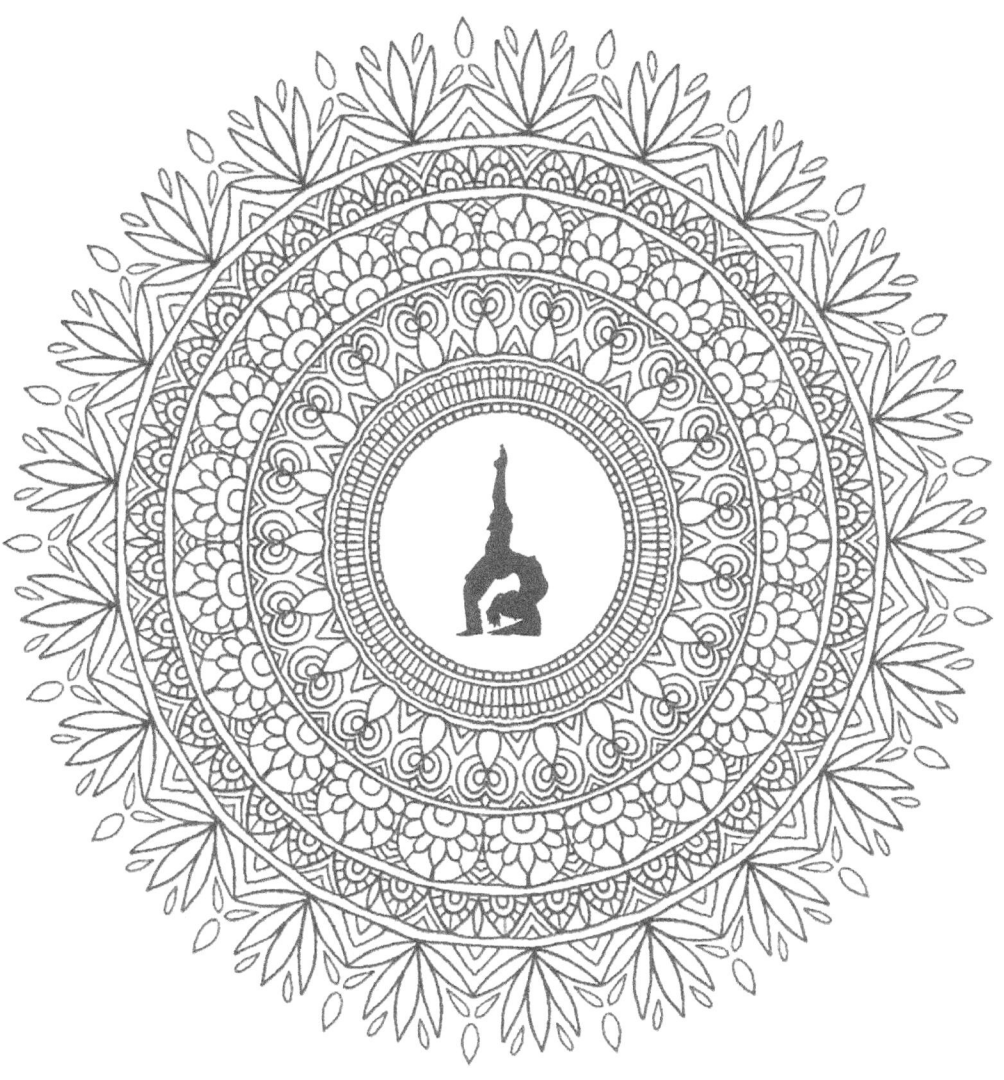

Purity or impurity depends on oneself. No one can purify another. ~ The Buddha

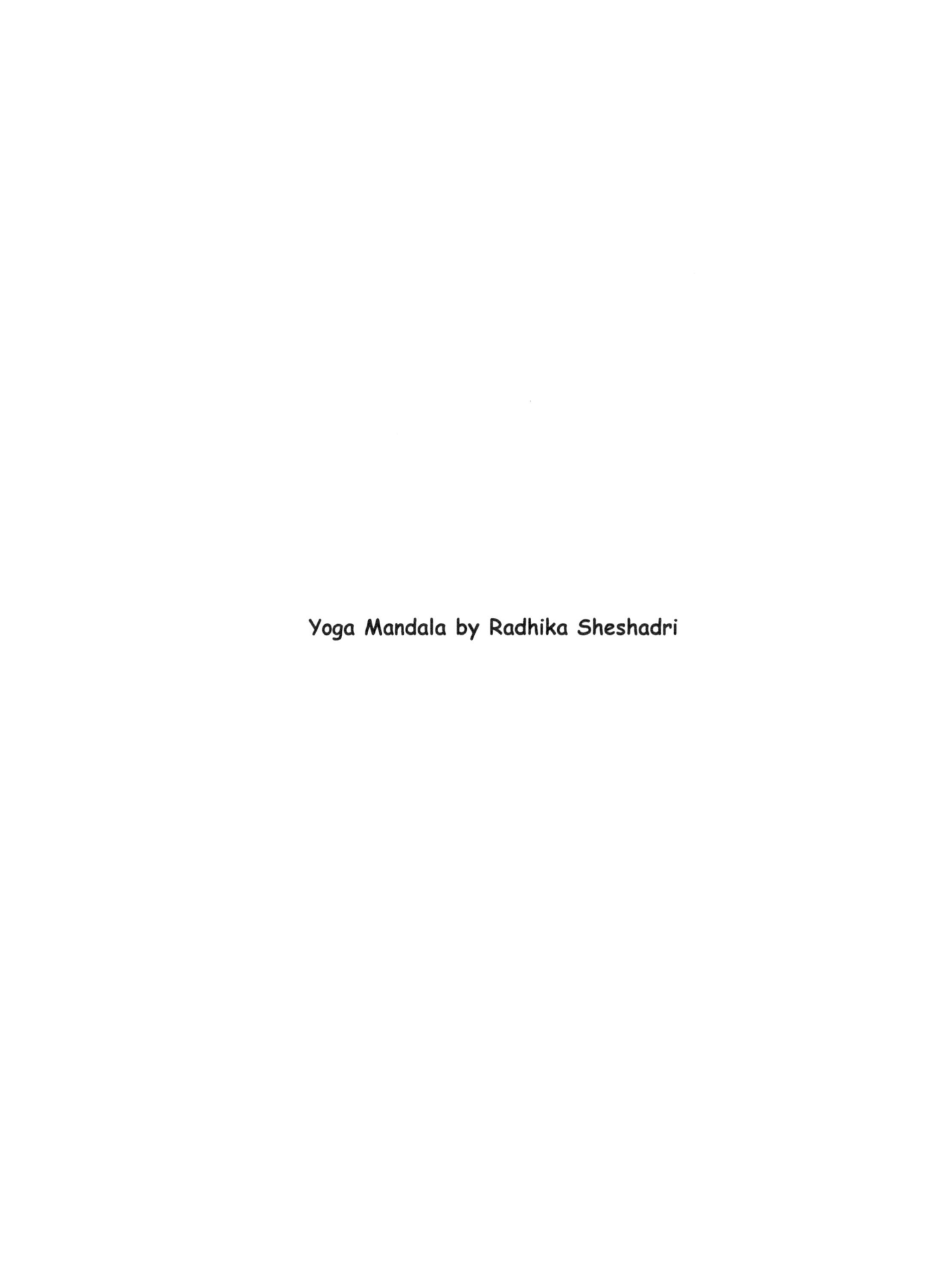

Yoga Mandala by Radhika Sheshadri

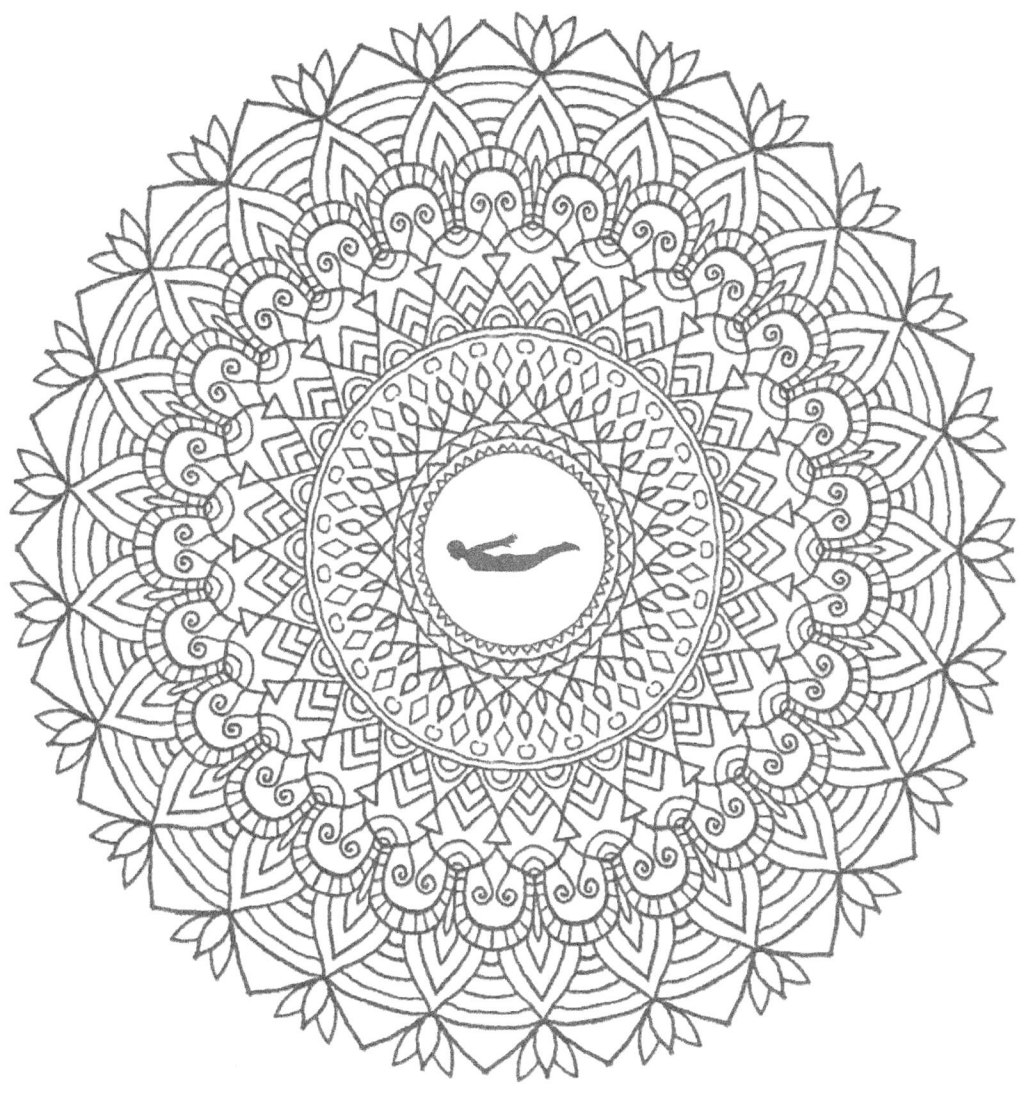

To conquer oneself is a greater task
than conquering others. ~ The Buddha

Yoga Mandala by Radhika Sheshadri

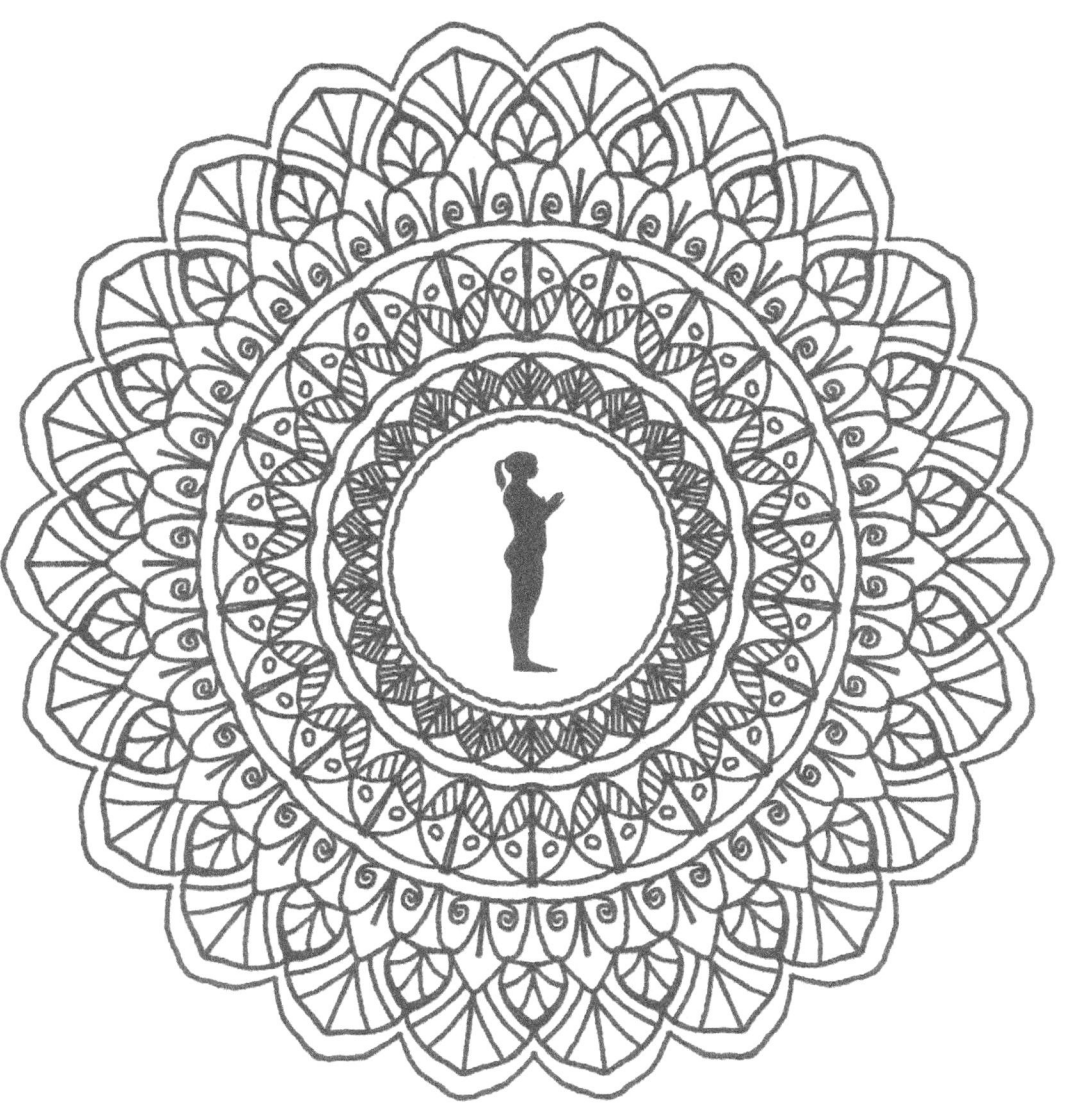

Thousands of candles can be lighted from a single candle, and the life of the candle will not be shortened. Happiness never decreases by being shared. ~The Buddha

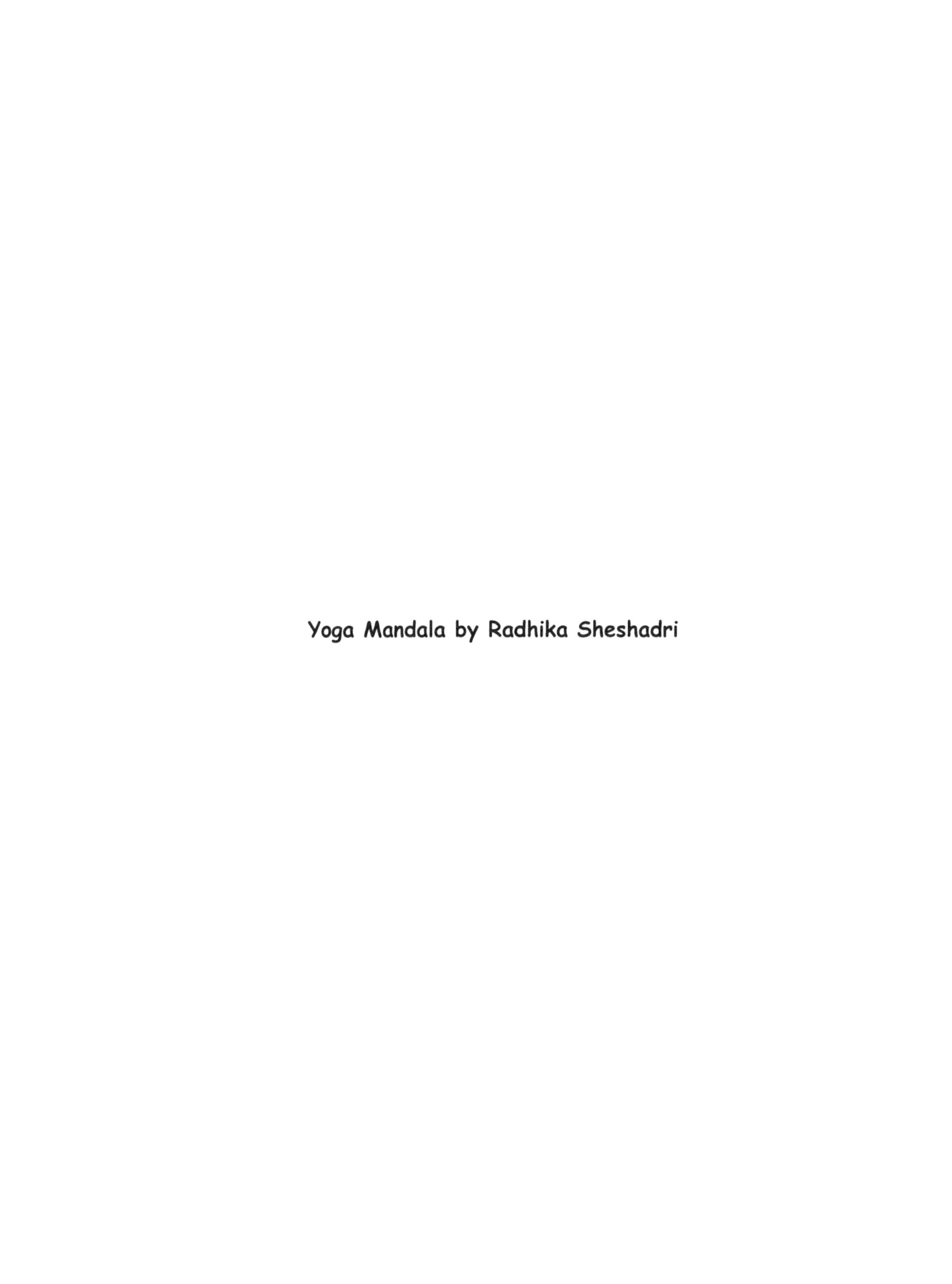

Yoga Mandala by Radhika Sheshadri

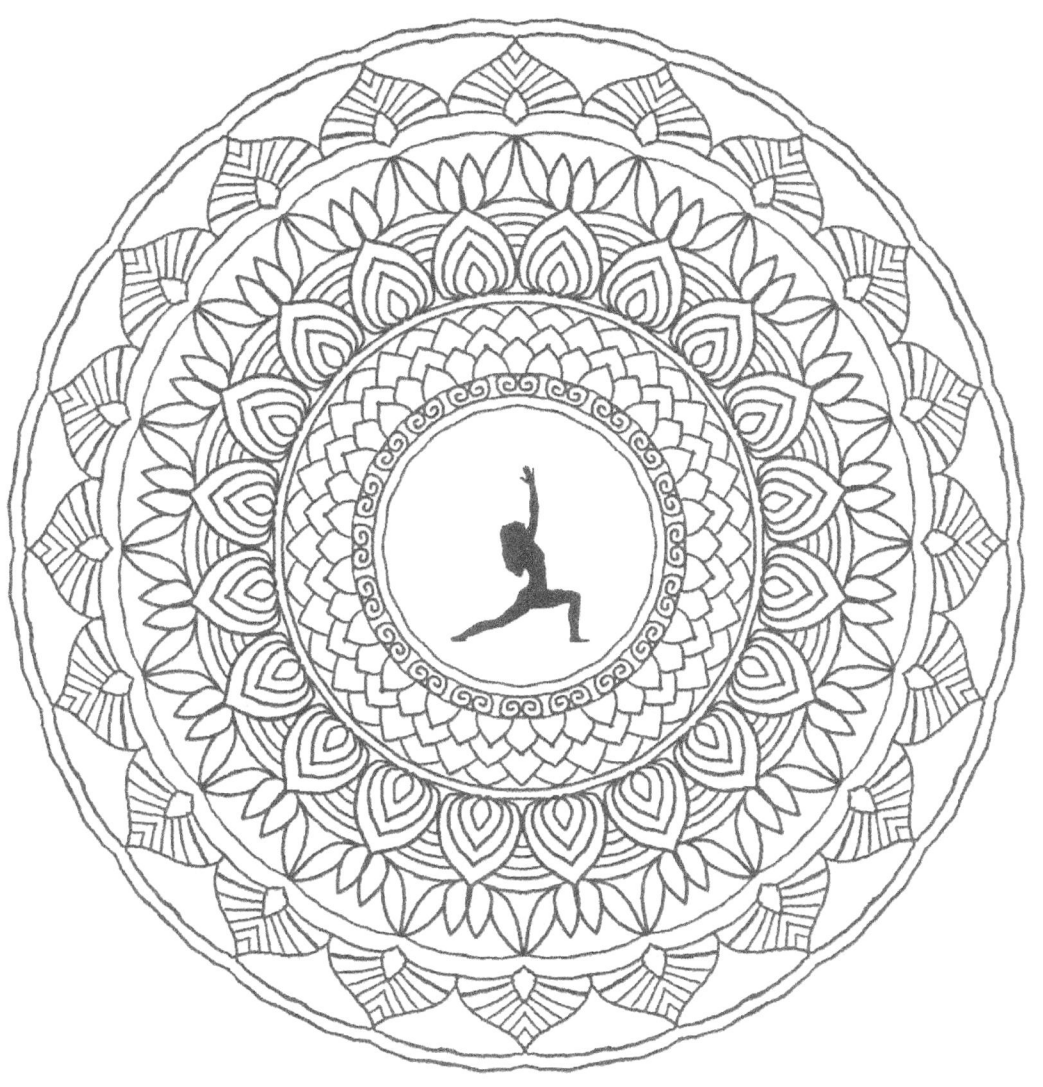

Do not dwell in the past, do not dream of the future, concentrate the mind on the present moment.~The Buddha

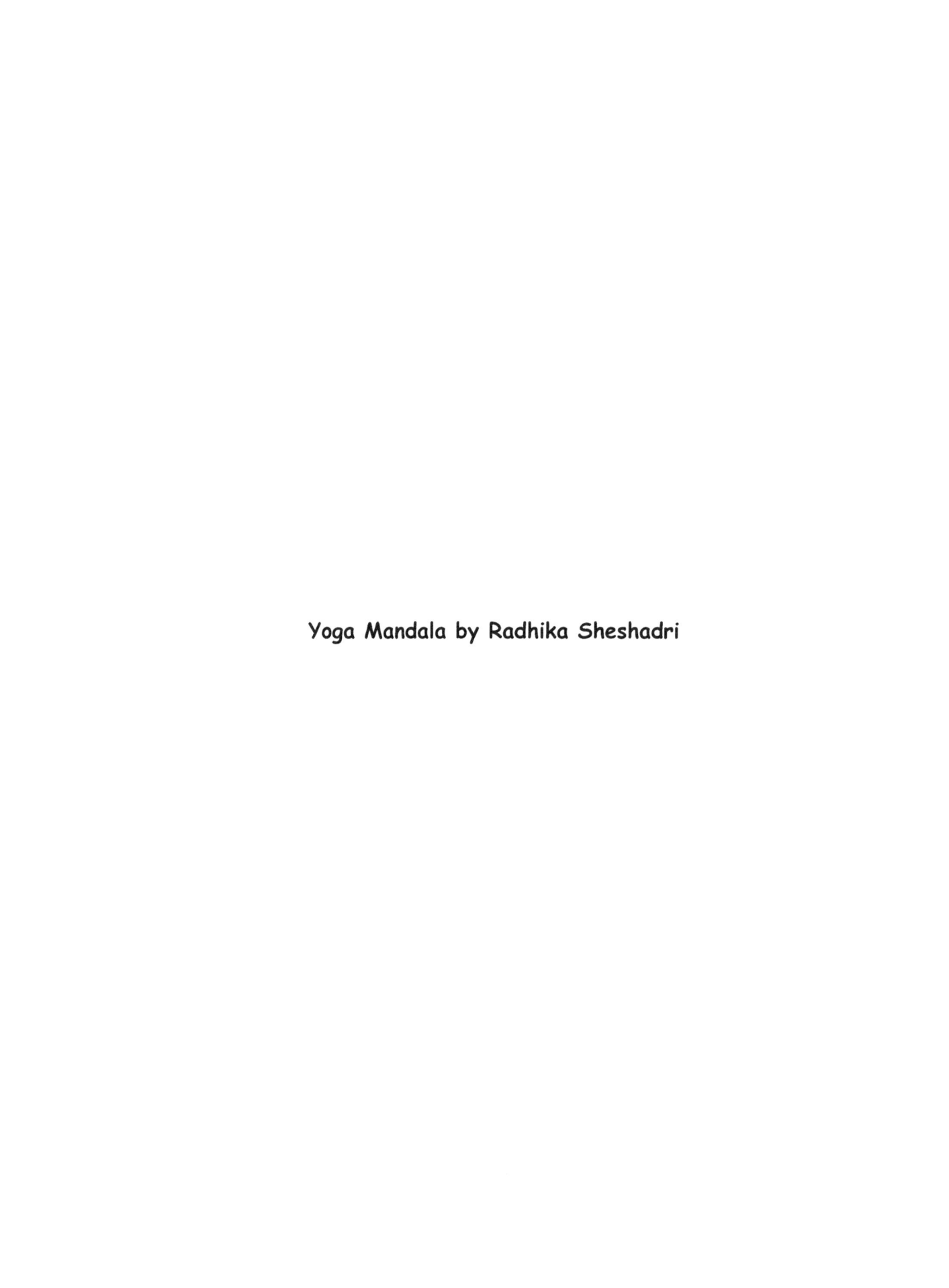

Yoga Mandala by Radhika Sheshadri

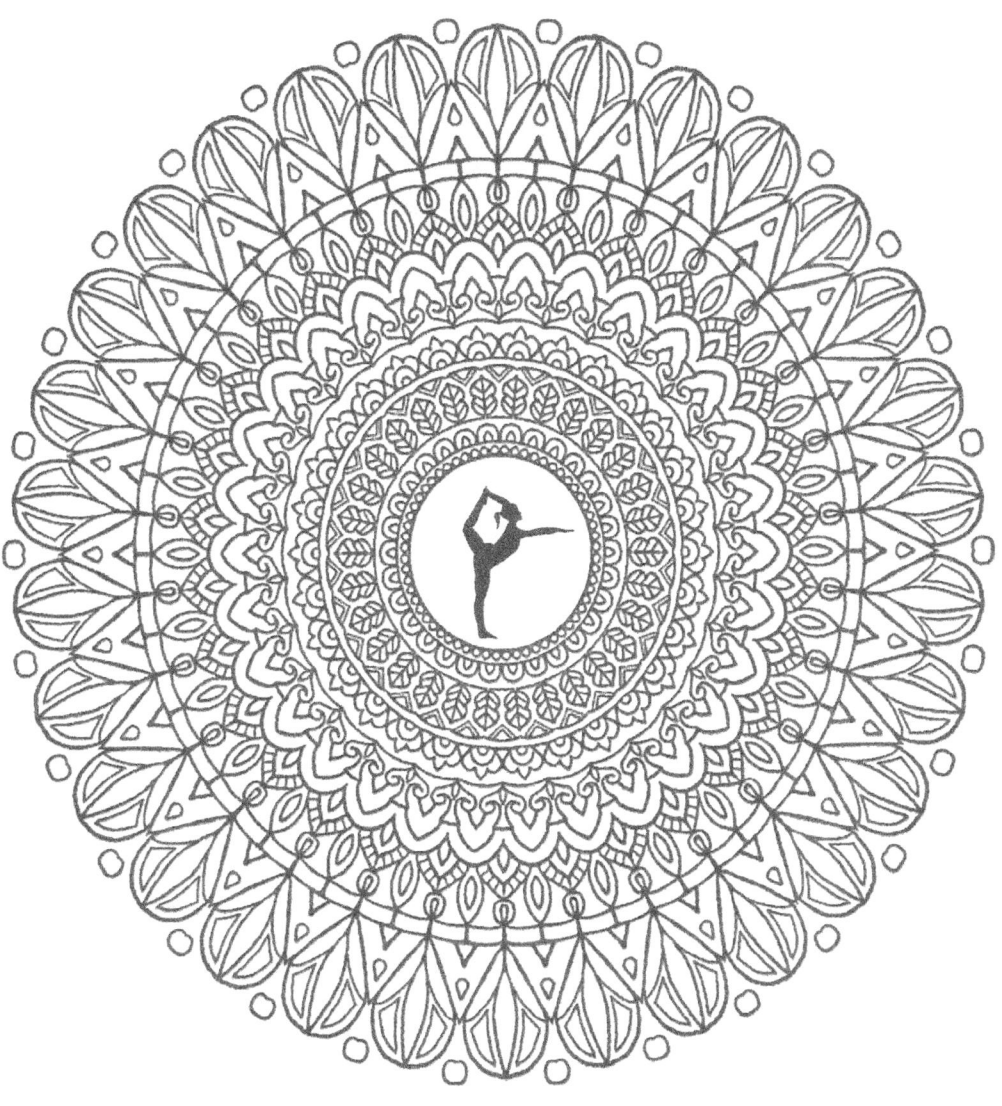

We are shaped by our thoughts; we become what
we think. When the mind is pure, joy follows like
a shadow that never leaves.~Buddha

Yoga Mandala by Radhika Sheshadri

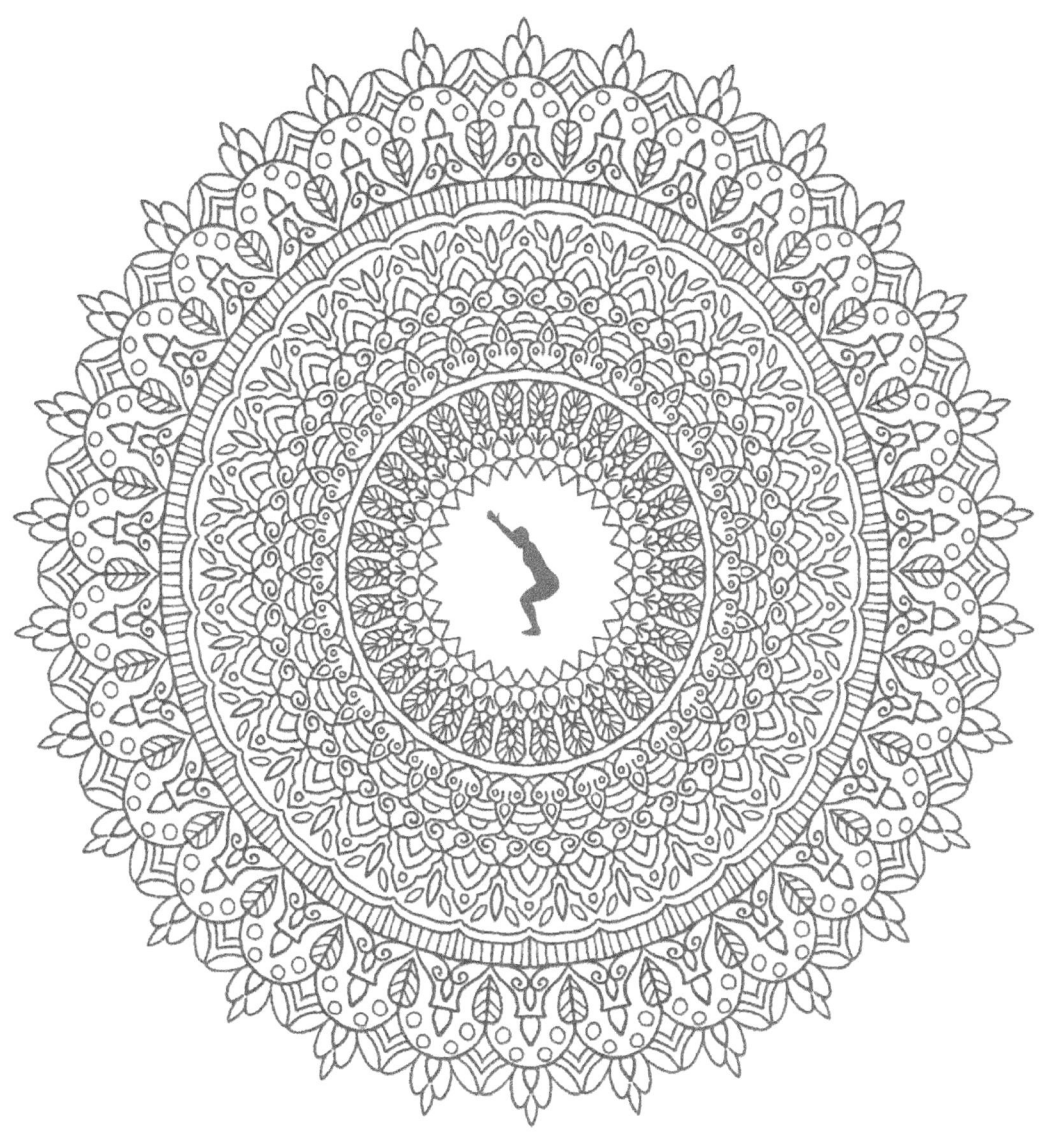

Just as a snake sheds its skin, we must shed our
past over and over again. ~ The Buddha

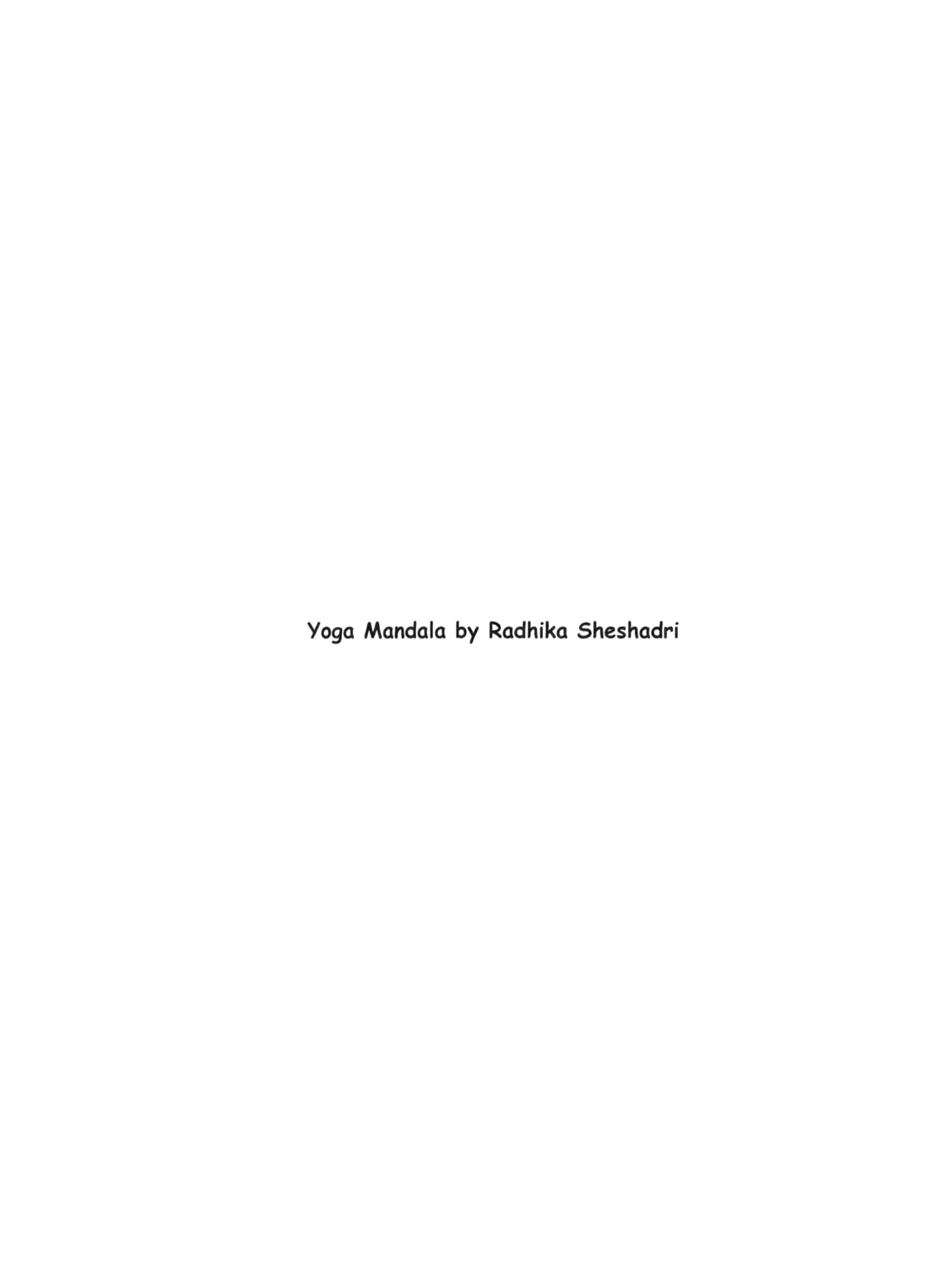

Yoga Mandala by Radhika Sheshadri

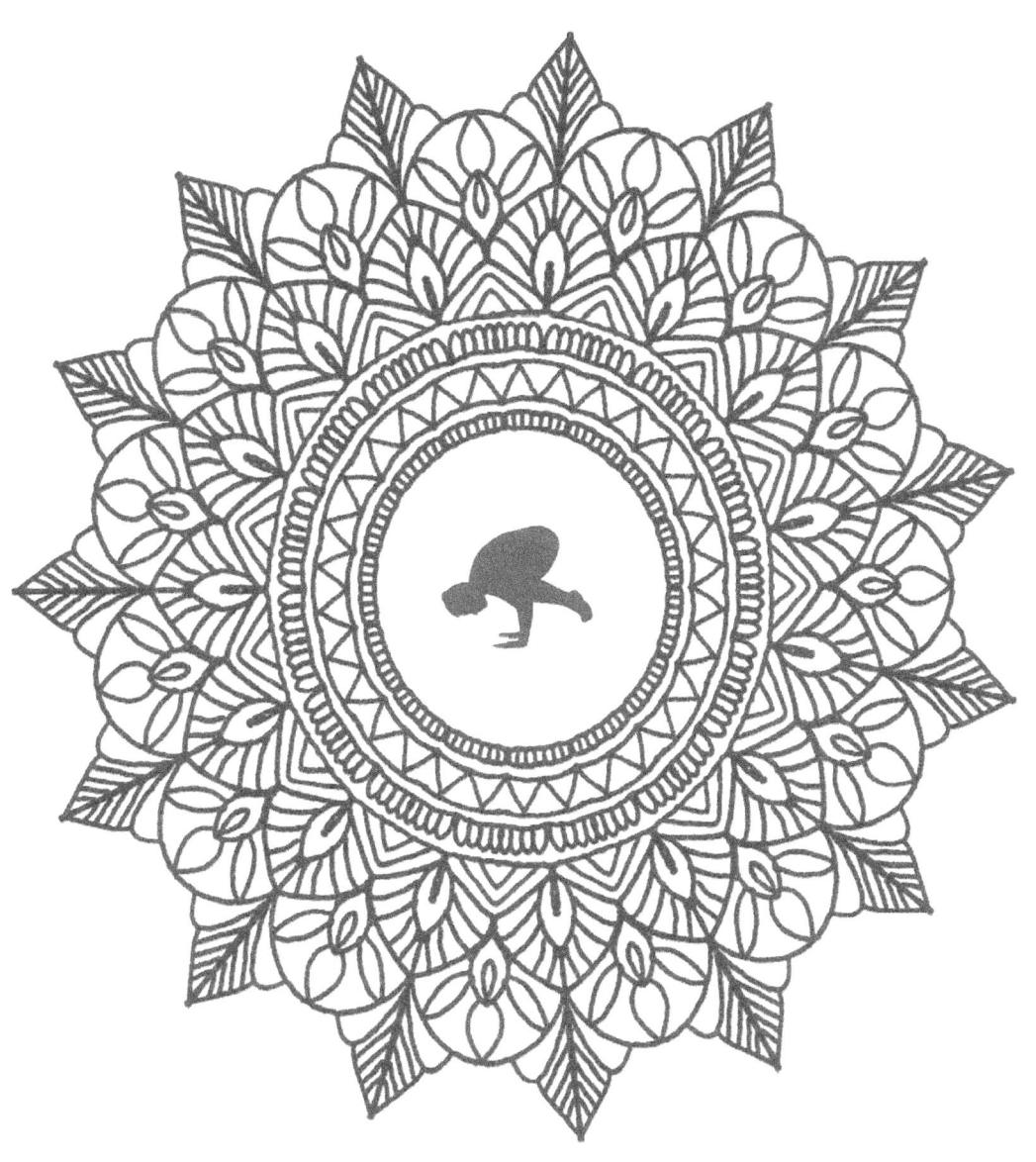

Whatever words we utter should be chosen with care for people will hear them and be influenced by them for good or ill. ~The Buddha

Yoga Mandala by Radhika Sheshadri

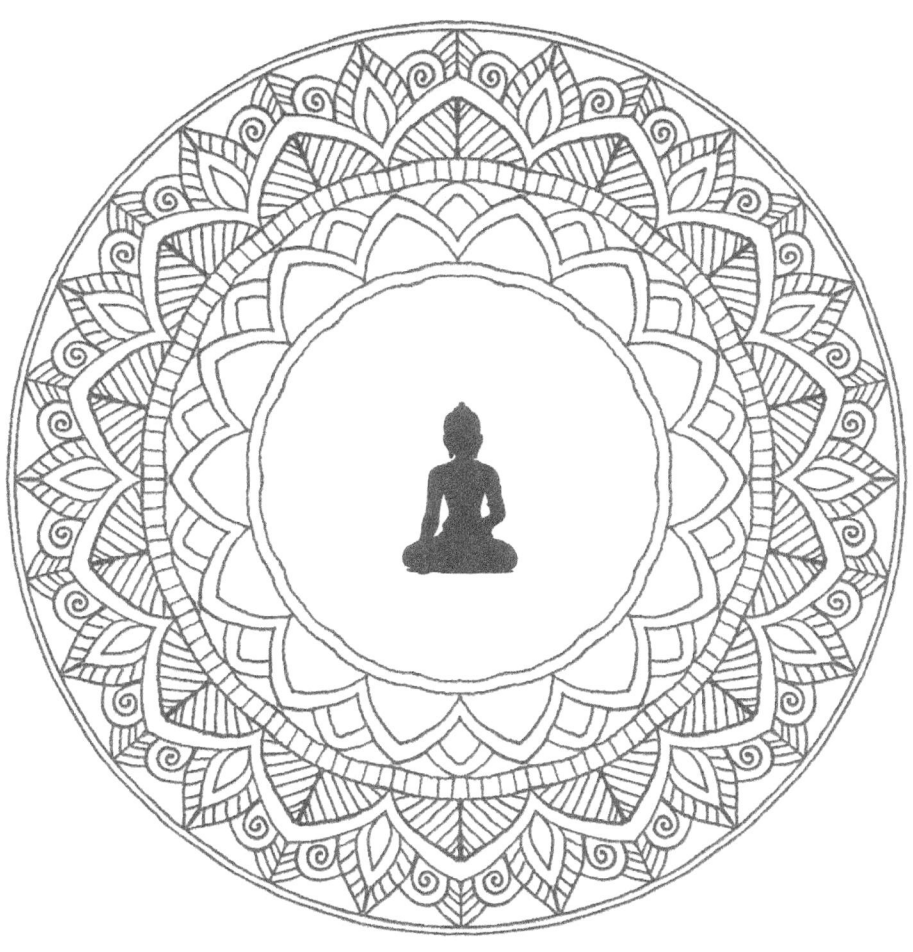

If with a pure mind a person speaks or acts, happiness follows them like a never-departing shadow.~The Buddha

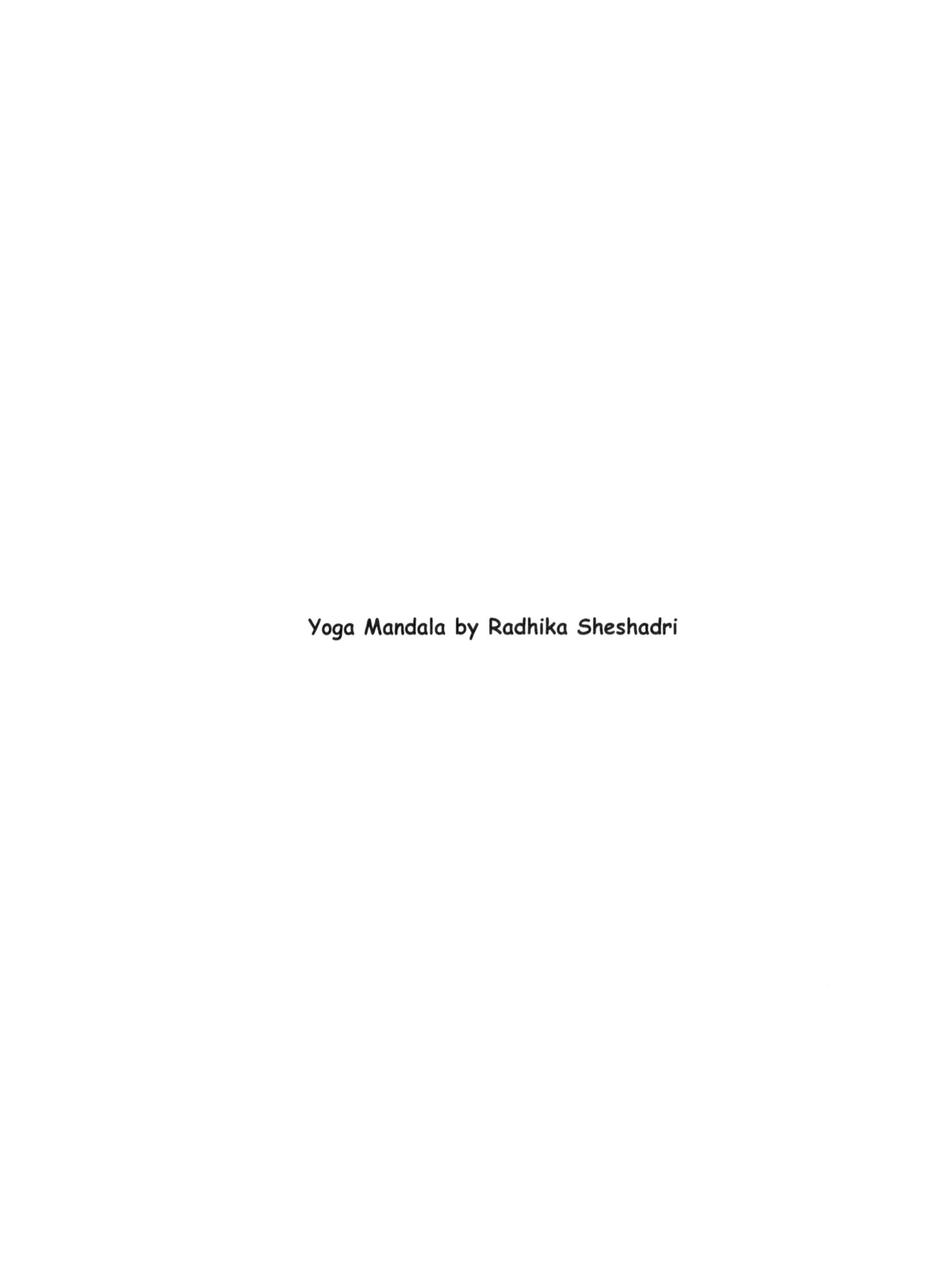

Yoga Mandala by Radhika Sheshadri

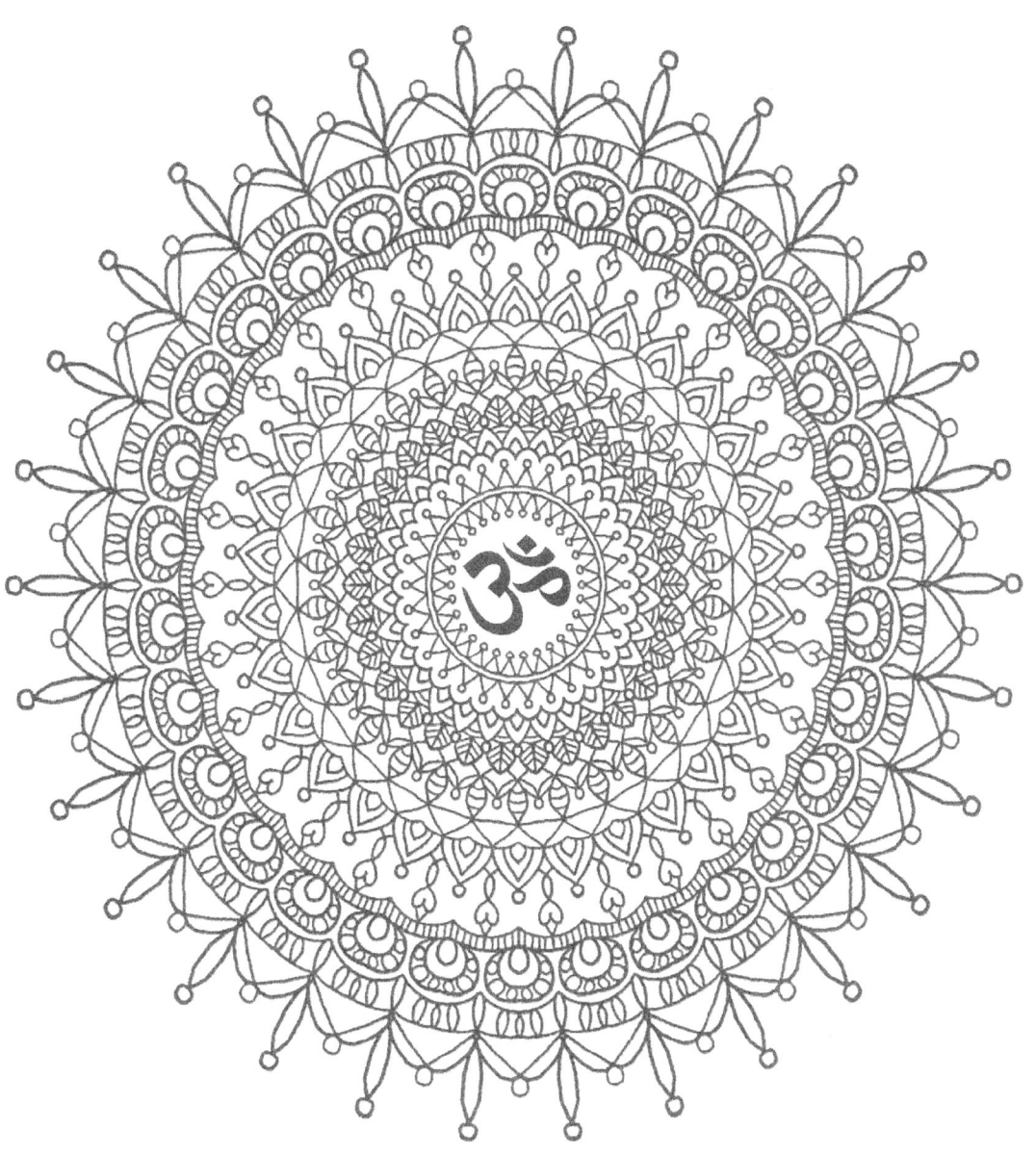

If we could see the miracle of a single flower clearly, our whole life would change. ~ The Buddha

Yoga Mandala by Radhika Sheshadri

www.ingramcontent.com/pod-product-compliance
Lightning Source LLC
Chambersburg PA
CBHW081910170526
45167CB00007B/3225